D0571559

CAREERS FOR
WOMEN AS
CLERGY

By
Rev. JULIE F. PARKER

The Rosen Publishing Group, Inc.
NEW YORK

Published in 1993 by The Rosen Publishing Group, Inc.
29 East 21st Street, New York, NY 10010

First Edition

Library of Congress Cataloging-in-Publication Data

Parker, Julie F.
    Careers for women as clergy / by Julie F. Parker. — 1st ed.
        p.   cm.
    Includes bibliographical references and index.
    Summary: Examines the opportunites for religious service,
including ordination as ministers and rabbis, that are open to
women and discusses role models and finding one's "calling."
    ISBN 0-8239-1424-0   ISBN 0-8239-1727-4 (pbk)
    1. Women clergy—Vocational guidance—Juvenile
literature. [1. Women clergy—Vocational guidance.
2. Clergy—Vocational guidance. 3. Vocational guidance.]
I. Title.
BV676.P29 1993
253'.2'082—dc20   93-18228
                                                        CIP
                                                        AC

Manufactured in the United States of America

To
my parents, Merolyn and David,
and to my husband, Bill,
with love and thanks beyond words

Acknowledgments

Writing this book has been a pleasure because it has enabled me to come in contact with many women whom I find fascinating. I would like to thank the Jewish, Protestant, and Roman Catholic women from across the country who contributed their insights to this book. They are:

Rev. Nancy Adams, Ms. Marilyn Alexander, Rabbi Rebecca Alpert, Rev. Danita Anderson, Rev. Esther Angel, Rev. Karen Barker-Duncan, Rev. Caroline Berninger, Ms. Helen Betenbaugh, Rev. Cynthia Biddlecomb, Rabbi Barbara Borts, Dr. Lillian Bozak-Deleo, Rev. Marjorie Bradshaw, Ms. Theresa Brophy, Rev. LaTaunya Bynum, Rabbi Debra Cantor, Rabbi Nina Cardin, Rev. Sally Ruggia Chapin, Rev. Colleen Chun, Rev. Jungrea Chung, Ms. Janet Comperry, Rabbi Rachel Cowan, Rev. Jean Lofsvold Cress, Rev. Gail Crouch, Rev. Jean Dix, Rev. Mary Dye, Rev. Catherine Ellenwood, Ms. Linda Nash Engleby, Ms. Cass Englert, Rev. Judith Favor, Rev. Jane Ferguson, Rabbi Lori Forman, Ms. Sharon Forman, Ms. Rebecca Garfein, Rabbi Rosalind Gold, Sr. Elaine Goodell, Rev. Martha Green, Rev. Anne Griffith, Rabbi Susan Grossman, Rev. Peggy Gunness, Rev. Kay Hereford, Rev. Bonna Sue Himes, Dr. Mary Hunt, Cantor Jenny Izenstark, Rev. Marguerite Jhonson, Rev. Kathi Jones, Rabbi Debra Joselow, Rev. Eunhae Kee, Sr. Margie Kelly, Rev. Doris Kinton, Rev. Dr. Lois Kirkwood, Ms. Laurie Knutsen, Rabbi Lynne Landsberg, Rev. Agnes Lasetchuk, Rev. Suk Jong Lee, Ms. Susan Leet,

Rev. Kate Lehman, Rabbi Joy Levitt, Rev. Dr. Judy Lindsey, Rev. Sharon Link, Rev. Susan Lloyd-Pearce, Ms. Vicky Luna, Rev. Patsy Kelly Mack, Rabbi Janet Marder, Sr. Dorothy Marnell, Rev. Linda McCrae, Rev. Julia Athinson Melgreen, Rev. Sue Ellen Miller, Sr. Mary Moynihan, Rev. Sondra Newman, Cantor Martha Novick, Rev. Karen Oliveto, Rev. Katherine Thomas Paisley, Rev. Kate Parker-Burgard, Rev. Guylan Gail Paul, Rev. Bonnie Perry, Rev. Janet Porcher, Rev. Jeanne Audrey Powers, Rabbi Sally Priesand, Ms. Katherine Ragsdale, Rev. Karen Sapio, Rabbi Sandy Eisenberg Sasso, Rev. Mariellen Sawada, Rev. Lynn Scott, Ms. Mary Serovy, Rev. Kyung-Lim Shin-Lee, Rabbi Marion Shulevitz, Rev. Laura Sinclair, Rev. Kristen Soltvedt, Rev. Joan Speaks, Rabbi Reena Spicehandler, Ms. Christy Stanton, Ms. Susan Steinberg, Rabbi Shira Stern, Rev. Charlotte Still, Rev. Dr. Cathy Stonehouse, Rev. Felicia Thomas, Rev. Dr. Carolyn Tyler-Benson, Ms. Elizabeth Verdesi, Rev. Lillian Frier Webb, Rev. Alicia Fils-Aime Wentler, Rev. Traci West, Rev. Odella Williamson, Rev. Suanne Williams-Wliorl, Rev. Marcia Smith Wood, and Rev. Rachel Chung Sook Ye.

Many thanks to Ms. Ann Burrows, Rev. Dolores Henderson, Rabbi Linda Henry Goodman, and the East Meadow United Methodist Church for participating in the creation of the cover photo.

Special thanks go to Rev. Laura Benson and Rabbi Linda Henry Goodman for their helpful suggestions.

Other friends and colleagues generously gave their time through interviews and insights: Jeffrey Gibelius, Ken Guest, Barbara Millman, Rabbi Meir Mitelman, Rev. David Parker, Rabbi Larry Raphael, Rev. Craig Settlage, and Rabbi Gerry Serotta.

At the Rosen Publishing Group, Roger Rosen and Jeff Donaldson-Forbes have been helpful and encouraging throughout the project. I am also very grateful to Greg Blue for thinking that this book would be an important addition to the Career series and that I might be a good person to write it.

I would like to thank my family and friends, especially Merolyn Graham Parker, Maureen Horowitz-Coffin, and Mark Coffin, for the precious gifts of time. Thanks also to my sister Valerie for all the calls. My husband, Bill Crawford, offers constant loving support and keeps me laughing so I don't take myself too seriously. And finally, heartfelt appreciation goes to our baby, Graham David. His gestation and formation largely coincided with that of this book, and he helped me as much as he could *in utero* by gifting me with a fairly easy pregnancy.

About the Author

Rev. Julie Parker

Julie Parker is an ordained minister in the United Methodist Church. She has been active in the church throughout her life; her father is also a Methodist minister, as is one of her two younger sisters.

A graduate of Hamilton College, she pursued theological studies at Union Theological Seminary in New
York City, where she received a Master of Divinity
degree. During her undergraduate and graduate years
she studied art history in Paris, and theology in San
José, Costa Rica. She has published articles in English
and Spanish on her studies abroad, popular culture,
and theology.

Her professional experience includes work on the
campus ministry staffs of American University and
George Washington University, both in Washington
D.C. She also was a pastor of a church on Long Island.
Currently she serves as the Protestant Chaplain at
Hofstra University, Hempstead, New York, and teaches
on the theology faculty of Molloy College, Rockville
Centre, New York. Her interests include karate, drama,
and marathon running. She is married to Rev. Bill
Crawford, pastor of the First Presbyterian Church in
Freeport, New York, where they live with their son,
Graham.

Contents

Preface

Growing up as the daughter of a minister, I remember my school friends asking me what my father did all week. "Doesn't he work for just an hour on Sundays?" I vividly recall one sixth-grade girl inquiring. Although I knew then that clergy, like my dad, were very busy, it was not until I became a minister myself that I began to appreciate how full a clergyperson's life is. This book is written to help you explore the fullness of a clergy-woman's life—professionally and personally—so you can investigate whether the career might be right for you.

Since there are countless religious faiths and organizations in the United States, this book focuses primarily on certain traditions. Among Christian churches, I concentrate on mainline (or mainstream) Protestant denominations such as the American Baptist, Disciples of Christ, Episcopal, Evangelical Lutheran Church in America, Presbyterian Church (USA), United Church of Christ, and United Methodist churches. Among branches of Judaism, I discuss the Reform, Reconstructionist, and Conservative movements, since those traditions ordain women. Although most attention on Jewish clergy is given to rabbis, cantors are also clergy and are discussed separately. Because Roman Catholicism is so prominent in this country (comprising over one quarter of the population), stories of Roman Catholic women are included in Chapter 2, and Catholic women in chapters where the career choice that is discussed is currently available to them.

Although women in Roman Catholicism, Orthodox

Judaism, and various other faith traditions are not currently ordained, the purpose of this book is not to argue for the ordination of women. Not surprisingly, I believe that ordination is the privilege and responsibility of those who are called and compelled to serve in this way and are capable of the challenges, regardless of gender. And as more and more women become ministers, rabbis, and cantors—women like you—clergywomen are increasingly accepted and appreciated.

Many clergywomen of various religious, racial, and geographic backgrounds have contributed their insights to this book. They are of different ages and handicapping conditions; some have years of experience as clergy, others are new in their careers or are still working toward ordination. Through phone conversations, personal interviews, and more than a hundred questionnaires, women shared their stories of what led them to their career, what they do, what they like best, what they like least, and what advice they would offer future clergywomen. (A copy of the questionnaires can be found in the Appendix.) With the help of their input, I have outlined these careers for women as clergy in the hope that the practical information and their honest reflections will lead you to your own decisions and discoveries.

1

Striding into the Future

If you are a young woman considering a career in clergy, you were born at the right time! Never before have there been so many opportunities for women as ministers, rabbis, and cantors (or clergy) as there are now. The chances are pretty good that being ordained, which is being given authority as a clergyperson, has been an option for you throughout your life. You may have grown up hearing a woman preach from the pulpit in your congregation and thought to yourself that this was something you might want to do someday. Perhaps someone you know was in the hospital, and the chaplain who came to visit was a woman. Maybe a clergywoman officiated at a wedding you attended. Even if you do not know a woman who is a minister or rabbi, you may have learned from your friends, community, or the media that clergywomen are thriving in their positions and growing in number. Today there are more than twenty thousand clergywomen in our country. Only a generation ago, almost all clergy were men.

In some faith traditions, notably the Roman Catholic Church and Orthodox Judaism, the ranks of the clergy are still closed to women. Some people in these traditions are working to change this so that future women might be ordained. Currently, however, other career options are open to Catholic and Orthodox women who feel called to serve God and their community of faith. If you are a young Roman Catholic or Orthodox Jewish woman considering a career as a clergywoman, know that your contributions would be welcomed, encouraged, and valued in many areas of religious work, although becoming a priest or rabbi is not a possibility now. Although most of this book is devoted to the Protestant and Jewish traditions that do ordain women, many of the career options outlined here are also available to you.

In most Protestant denominations and Jewish movements, the number of women ministers and rabbis has grown enormously over the past few decades. In one way, that should not be surprising because previously women were denied ordination. A few Protestant denominations have been ordaining women since the nineteenth century, such as the American Baptist Churches (ordaining women for over one hundred years), the Disciples of Christ (1888), and the United Church of Christ (1853). In these denominations, decision-making lies largely with the local congregation, and as a result a few exceptional women were ordained that long ago. Other denominations bound by a national governing system began fully ordaining women (without regional restrictions) in the late 1950s and early '60s. Among them are the Presbyterian Church in the United States (1964) and the United Presbyterian Church (1956), now combined into the Presbyterian Church (USA), and the United Methodist Church (1956). In the 1970s the Lutheran Church in America and the American Lutheran Church (now combined into the Evangelical Lutheran Church in America) started ordaining women, and in 1974 the first women were ordained as priests in the Episcopal Church. In Judaism, the Reform movement was the first to ordain a woman as a rabbi (1972), with the Reconstructionist movement closely following in 1974. The first woman Conservative rabbi was ordained in 1985.

Now that many doors are open, women are pouring into the ranks of the clergy in rapidly growing numbers. In the past few decades, many women who had been engaged in other careers, perhaps as homemakers, nurses, teachers, or social workers, turned to the ministry in midlife and developed it as their second career. Younger women especially had the chance to develop a career as a clergywoman upon graduation from college. This sharply rising trend of women deciding to become clergy is reflected in the number of female students at seminaries.

For Protestants, as recently as the 1970s only about ten percent of the students in seminary were women. In the 1990s women comprise more than half the students at larger interdenominational seminaries and across the board constitute a third of those seeking ordination in mainline Protestant churches. Nearly half of the entering students in rabbinical classes in Reconstructionist, Reform, and Conservative seminaries are women. Although the Roman Catholic Church does not yet ordain women, women nonetheless are taking on new responsibilities and frequently have influential roles as parish associates, preachers, youth ministers, liturgists, and eucharistic ministers. With many of the nation's clergymen facing retirement in this next decade, the large entry of clergywomen into our churches and synagogues is a powerful force in shaping the future of organized religion in this country.

Not only is this an opportune era in history to consider the clergy as a profession, but it is also a formative period in your personal growth when it can be exciting to ponder what you might want to do later in your life.

3

Rev. Rachel Ye, a United Methodist pastor, preaches during Sunday morning worship.

Perhaps you recently became a *Bat Mitzvah*[1], and felt an inner stirring as you read from the *Torah* (the first five books of the Bible) that caused you to wonder if you should become a rabbi. Possibly you went on a spiritual retreat with your church youth group and came back with renewed dedication to your Christian faith that prompted you to think about becoming a minister. You may have spent a summer in Israel that made you want to immerse yourself in the study of Judaism. Maybe when you were confirmed you enjoyed studying the Scriptures and preparing for the day of your confirmation; you may have thought that you might want to spend more of your life learning about your tradition and teaching others. If you are active in your church or synagogue youth group, you may realize that you have leadership talent. Your personal and spiritual questions may bring you to search your soul about God, your faith, and what you should do with your life. Those who become clergy are motivated by these and thousands of other reasons. But to start exploring career options while you are in school gives you a tremendous advantage as you decide whether becoming a clergywoman may be right for you.

Many religious and practical questions may come up as you consider this profession. For instance, "How do I become a minister or rabbi?" "Is this what God wants me to do?" "How would I get started?" "Whom can I talk to?" "How much schooling is required?" "How much would I be likely to earn?" "How hard is it to be a clergywoman and a mother?" "What is work as a clergywoman like?" This book is designed to help you find the answers to questions like those and to ask some

---

[1] *Bat/Bar Mitzvah* (Hebrew)—literally, daughter or son of the commandment, a ritual of passage for a girl or boy about thirteen years old, signifying entrance into adulthood.

personal questions of yourself. The thoughts and comments of clergywomen of various religious faiths are recounted here, so that their insights may lead you to your own. Regardless of where you are in your spiritual and professional quest, you are interested enough to be reading this book. You are already taking a step on your career journey.

As you learn about becoming a clergywoman, you will come to realize that in many ways this career is like lots of others. Being a minister or rabbi demands skills that need training to acquire and practice to develop. You need to fulfill specific educational requirements. You report to your office and have a busy schedule of meetings and appointments. You may be concerned about your salary and raises. Strategies about your next move can be pivotal. Relationships with colleagues are important. You may experience discrimination because of who you are and how you look. The demands on your time are great. At moments it may seem that there is little appreciation for what you do. At other times you may be outwardly excited or quietly content with all that you have accomplished. These attributes describe many careers—being a minister or rabbi is certainly among them.

But in some ways, being a clergyperson is a career unlike any other. You become a "professional" Christian or Jew, employed to uphold your faith tradition and share it with others. Expectations of a minister or rabbi are very high. There is rarely a nine-to-five schedule: The position is full-time in the truest sense of the word. Not only are you expected to work well, but you are also looked to for moral standards in how you live your life. For better or worse (usually worse), people often think of you as God's representative. Wherever people in the community run into you, be it in a grocery store, a post office, or on the street, they look at you and see "the rabbi" or "the minister." It's more than a job; it's an identity.

The career is highly public. Upon moving into a position, you become known in the community with almost celebrity status. People come to you with their most heartfelt concerns, even though they may never have met you before. Through your role, you are trusted and respected for your knowledge, training, and spirituality. You are turned to as an authority to offer guidance and to provide leadership. At times the public responsibilities seem overwhelming.

But the career is intensely personal as well. At the heart of what you do is your relationship with God. You are called on to share precious matters of faith. Prayer and devotion are part of your daily routine. Your love of God and people needs to be strong and honest. Yet when you are helping others, the private rewards of knowing that you are also serving God offer a deep satisfaction and make you grateful for the chance to be a rabbi or minister.

Being a clergyperson is different for women than for men in many ways. For many congregations, having a clergywoman is still a deviation from the norm. Some people may be shocked to discover that their new minister or rabbi is not a man, and initially they may be unsure how to respond to a clergywoman. Hospital patients may be surprised when the chaplain with a clerical collar who comes to visit them is a woman. Some people may be curious to hear how a woman's voice sounds preaching from the pulpit or singing as a cantor. Some are jolted by the image of a clergyperson who is pregnant. Even those who might not think twice about going to a woman doctor or consulting a female lawyer might be upset at the idea of having a woman minister or rabbi. This is partly because having numerous clergywomen is still relatively new, and partly because the

7

presence of women as clergy raises many questions about traditional religion.

Many people think of their clergyperson as a representative of God, and often God is depicted as male. Although believers are taught that God is a spirit and without gender, most of the powerful images and figures that remind people of God and God's power, from Moses to the Pope, are also male. To encounter a woman in a position of religious leadership can feel very threatening to one's beliefs and religious life. It may seem as if the rock of tradition, solid and steadfast, is beginning to crumble.

But clergywomen view this period in religious history as a time to continue building the strength and vitality of our churches and synagogues while expanding the image of what a clergyperson is really like. Although it would be unfair and inaccurate to categorize all clergymen one way and all clergywomen another, it is clear that women do bring new dimensions to the ministry. Some clergywomen's vocational goals may be different from those of many of their male colleagues. For example, some may concentrate less on ascending the career ladder and more on the quality of relationships where they are. Clergywomen who are mothers give priority to spending time with their families. Often clergywomen boldly take on issues of sexuality and openly address the problems of rape, sexual harassment, and domestic violence. Some clergywomen develop creative worship services to help people discover new ways to feel closer to God. Many clergywomen emphasize sharing power and making decisions together with the people of their congregations. Women in the ministry who have experienced discrimination themselves may be led to work against all forms of discrimination and to develop an inclusive theology. Clergywomen also realize the need for support in these pioneering times and gather in formal and informal groups to share their concerns, joys, and frustrations. While varying from one individual to the next, women bring their own concerns, styles, and contributions to their roles as clergy.

As women do this, people come to realize that a clergyperson's ability to fulfill her or his responsibilities depends more on the person than the person's gender. Clergywomen gain respect, and new generations find nothing unusual about ministers or rabbis who are women. Many clergywomen share stories similar to that of one pastor who tells about what happened in her church one Sunday morning. At the start of the worship service, she was processing up the aisle behind the choir. As she passed by a pew, a little boy tugged at his mother's sleeve and asked, "Mommy, can men be ministers too?"

As people's image of a clergyperson changes, new paths are being cut by women who expand the ideas of who a clergyperson is and contribute to the understanding of what she does. In whatever field you may someday choose, being a clergyperson would allow you the opportunity to incorporate your personality, talents, and abilities into your career. At the same time, you could help others as you live out your faith. Becoming a clergywoman may offer you the chance for a fulfilling, challenging, and ultimately rewarding career.

2

Sisters Who Helped Pave the Way

As long as there have been communities of faith, there have been women leading them. Throughout religious history, women have gathered with others to share their beliefs and speak their convictions. They have given their time, energy, talent, and resources to build up their communities. Passing down values and teaching customs to children has long been part of women's role to assure that their traditions endure. That women are crucial to the survival of their communities of faith is not a new phenomenon. What is revelatory, and even revolutionary, is that women now are moving into recognized positions of religious leadership in greater numbers than ever before.

For centuries, even millennia, women have not been allowed to attain positions of visible authority in their churches and synagogues. Reasons for this denial range from arguments about women's "weaker nature" and "inferior ability" to scriptural citations stating that women should obey men. Even though much of the Bible is understood as relevant to its own time thousands of years ago and not to our time—such as passages upholding slavery—verses saying that women should submit to men are still quoted as if they were timeless. Fortunately, such selective use of Scripture is often recognized today as a manipulation of the Bible to reinforce discrimination against women. However, as long as the education of women was a very low priority in society (as it has been until recently), women have not had the tools of knowledge that enable them to counter such prejudice effectively. Without access to education or positions of power, women have been severely disadvantaged in their struggles for equality.

Nonetheless, many resourceful women throughout the ages found their own ways to exercise influence and fulfill their call or desire to devote themselves to God and their faith community. These women struggled against tremendous odds, opposing the weight of cultural pressure that dictated that a woman's "proper" place was at home. In many cultures, an exemplary woman was expected to marry, then serve her husband and raise the children. Women who wanted to develop a career in religion worked hard to acquire an education, often with little formal schooling. They risked insult, harassment, and sometimes even their lives as they devoted themselves to their faith, following the inspiration that guided them despite possible persecution.

Here are glimpses of a few of the countless women who have helped to pave the way for Christian and Jewish women today while leaving their mark on American religious history. Many of their stories have been uncovered recently as feminist historians investigate the lives of previously forgotten women. Unfortunately, the brave witnesses of many more women are lost to us because information about them was never recorded. We can surmise, however, that the women whose voices we do hear echo the experiences of some of their contemporary sisters as they courageously held fast to their beliefs.

Anne Hutchinson (1591–1643)

As the first European settlers came to the "new world," they brought with them some old ideas about women. The medieval persecution of women as witches bred a distinct mistrust of women as sinful daughters of Eve. Education for women was considered especially dangerous. This belief system worked efficiently to keep women under control; to be outspoken was risky. Out of this context came Anne Hutchinson, an educated, outspoken woman.

Anne grew up in England as the daughter of a clergyman, who taught her to study and to understand the Bible. While in England, she married William Hutchinson, and the couple had fourteen children. Anne was a devout Christian and attended the services of the English Puritan minister John Cotton. The Puritans believed that some people were among "God's elect" and should worship simply, without religious vestments, stained-glass windows, or music. The archbishop of the Church of England wanted the Puritans silenced and had them thrown into prison. As a result of this persecution, many Puritans escaped to the colonies. Among them was the Hutchinson family, who braved the two-month voyage across the Atlantic in 1634, following John Cotton, who had made the trip the year before. Anne settled with her family in the Massachusetts Bay Colony, where she continued to attend the church of her minister from home.

Moved and inspired by Cotton's sermons, Anne invited women from the colony to her home twice a week to discuss the messages that they heard in church. These meetings rapidly became popular, with sixty to a hundred people attending regularly. At first they were looked upon with approval as helping to build up the church, but eventually Anne was perceived as a threat to the established government. She interpreted Cotton's sermons to emphasize grace as a personal experience between God and the individual; the Holy Spirit was the source of ultimate authority, rather than government officials or clergy. Not surprisingly, those in power did not approve of her point of view. Adding to their anger was the fact that their opponent was a woman, explaining her views in a way that they found highly inappropriate. They feared that she might encourage other women to speak their opinions. In November 1637 Anne Hutchinson was brought to trial for treason.

In the court proceedings, the fact that Anne was a woman was repeatedly raised against her. While Anne could defend herself biblically, in the mind of the judge, John Winthrop, who was also the prosecutor, her guilt was a foregone conclusion. In the spring of 1638, Anne was sentenced to excommunication from the congregation in Boston and banished from the colony.

This was a very harsh sentence, for excommunication forced Anne to leave the church, which was central to her life. Because there were few other settlements, banishment meant that Anne would have to transport her many children through unknown and dangerous areas. Even though she was fairly far along in another pregnancy, the Hutchinson family moved to Rhode Island. Anne subsequently gave birth to a baby who was badly deformed and dead at birth; proof, her critics claimed, that she had been "delivered up to Satan." After her husband's death in 1642, Anne heard rumors that the Puritans might buy Rhode Island. Fearing further religious persecution, she and her six youngest children moved to an area that was then "New Netherland," now Long Island. There she and all but one of her children died in an Indian attack in 1643.

Anne's story reveals a woman of remarkable conviction. She was independent, and her words and actions raised important questions about the status of women in colonial society. Taking risks themselves, many women supported her throughout her life, even moving their families with hers when she went to Rhode Island. Ironically, many of the Puritans who left England because of religious persecution in turn persecuted this Puritan woman for her beliefs. Anne Hutchinson's powerful witness of centuries ago gives us a courageous woman who, even in bitter hostility, exercised authority and held on to her strong spiritual beliefs.

Jarena Lee (1783-?)

Born when slavery was a strong institution in this country, Jarena Lee felt called to be a preacher. She faced great discrimination, not only because she was a woman, but also because she was black. Although her parents were free people living in New Jersey, they were forced by financial hardship to hire her out as a servant when she was seven years old. Gaining an education was a major obstacle for a black servant girl, but Jarena did not let that get in her way as she lived out her conviction to share the message of the Gospel. Eventually, she even published her autobiography, which has preserved her story for modern readers.

Jarena's personal life was intensely spiritual. At times she felt that she was such an awful sinner that she even contemplated suicide. Later in her life she interpreted those moments of doubt as the work of the devil. As a young adult, Jarena grew interested in becoming a Methodist and began attending worship services at Bethel African Methodist Episcopal Church in Philadelphia. There she was influenced by the sermons of the Reverend Richard Allen, who was the founder and senior minister of that church. While worshiping there, Jarena first felt the call to preach.

Although Jarena was clear that this was her mission,

the weight of such an awesome task felt overwhelming. She heard a voice say to her, "Go preach the Gospel!", to which she replied, "No one will believe me!" But the voice insisted that the right words would be put in her mouth. Jarena then began to dream of preaching before large crowds of people, and she would wake up from the sound of her own voice. When she told Mr. Allen of her desire to serve God as a preacher, she was gently informed that women could help in such areas as holding prayer meetings, but the rules of the church did not allow women preachers. Jarena told him that her Savior had died for the woman as well as the man, and she added, "Nothing is impossible with God."

During the next few years Jarena became diverted from her call to preach when she married a black pastor, Joseph Lee, in 1811. She moved to Snow Hill, a town a few miles outside of Philadelphia, where he was serving a church. There she often felt lonely, far from her home congregation. Over the next six years tragedy struck repeatedly, killing five members of her family, including her husband. In 1818, now as a single mother with two small children, Jarena Lee went back to Philadelphia.

She returned to her church and took on many responsibilities, visiting the sick and encouraging members to be more faithful. Still, Jarena described her desire to preach as "a fire shut up in my bones." At one service, it seemed clear to Jarena that the minister, the Reverend Mr. Williams, lacked the necessary inspiration. She sprang up from her seat and began preaching on the biblical passage that the minister had chosen. Richard Allen, who by this time had become a bishop, was present at this service. Instead of condemning Jarena's outspokenness, he publicly acknowledged that she was as capable of preaching as any of the clergy present. This launched the preaching career of Jarena Lee.

Jarena became a traveling preacher. Beginning in the

Philadelphia area, her work expanded as far south as Baltimore, Maryland, as far north as Rochester, New York, and as far west as Dayton, Ohio. Both blacks and whites came to hear her. Although Jarena was never licensed to preach nor ordained, her status as a "traveling exhorter" enabled her to deliver her message with the approval of the African Methodist Episcopal Church hierarchy. With the help of an editor, she wrote her autobiography, *The Life and Religious Experience of Jarena Lee*, and had it published in 1836. She passed out copies at religious meetings as a way to inspire others. In 1849 Jarena Lee published an expanded version of her autobiography, including information about her subsequent travels. After this, little is known of her life, but what we do know shows a woman of impressive vitality and strength.

Although Jarena's formal schooling totaled less than three months, she influenced thousands of people with her messages of hope and salvation. She believed this was the life that God intended for her. In spite of the discouragement of society, Jarena Lee trusted throughout her life that the Holy Spirit had called her to preach.

Sister Blandina (Rosa Maria Segale) (1850–1941)

The nineteenth century was a time of great expansion for this country and many of its institutions, including the Roman Catholic Church. Large numbers of Catholic immigrants contributed to the development of the Church in the United States. Many Catholic schools and hospitals were built. Despite frequent tension between Protestants and Catholics, many courageous Catholic women and men continued to shape their tradition despite discrimination.

Roman Catholic women at this time had two main options in life: become a mother, or become a nun.

The most common goal was to become a faithful wife and good mother, devoting oneself to taking care of one's husband and raising children in the Catholic faith. Women were expected to be obedient to men in nearly all circumstances. Although that was then the prevailing view in middle-class American society, Roman Catholics were often taught that the example of the Virgin Mary encouraged it as an ideal. Whereas wives could gain a certain status by trying to be like Mary, however, they were not supposed to act "improperly" for women. Voting, education, and employment outside the home were considered violations of the presumed "divine order" by which women were not to challenge men. Women were raised to believe that with religious observance went subservience.

The other option for Roman Catholic women, however, offered a radically different life-style from that of wife or mother. While requiring a commitment to chastity and the religious order, becoming a nun gave a Roman Catholic woman a chance for independence and freedom from the dominance of a husband and the responsibility of motherhood. Women who lived in a convent were part of a self-supporting community in which women were educated and held positions of power. Here they could develop their talents and leadership abilities. Nuns used their skills not only within the community, but also to contribute to society. Still, nuns often became targets of anti-Catholic sentiment, since they were easily recognized by their habit. Many nuns endured harsh treatment and difficult conditions as they lived out their calling.

One nun who faced many challenges and adventures was Sister Blandina. Born in Italy as Rosa Maria Segale, she went to live in Ohio, where she joined the Sisters of Charity in Cincinnati. At the age of twenty-two she traveled alone to the frontier in Colorado. There, in the town of Trinidad, she ran a public school with very limited resources. She gained the respect of the towns-people for her courage to speak her mind and to stand up for others. In an area where the rule of an angry mob often represented local "justice," Sister Blandina con-fronted gangs and interfered with their acts of violence.

On one particularly dangerous occasion, she foiled the plans of Billy the Kid. The bandit had planned to "scalp" the doctors of Trinidad for not removing a bullet from the leg of a member of his gang. However, Sister Blandina had been visiting the wounded man for months, and he had told her that the gang was planning a murder. When Billy and his gang came to town, Sister Blandina went to meet them. Billy said he had heard about her from the wounded man and offered to grant her a favor in thanks. When she requested that he spare the doctors' lives, Billy the Kid agreed. Sister Blandina's strength, while obviously very different from that of Billy the Kid, was certainly as powerful.

By defying convention, Sister Blandina and women like her helped people realize all that women could do. They refused to bow to the stereotype of women as meek and mild. Instead they continued doing what they understood as God's work, even though they risked personal harm. The bravery of religious women like Sister Blandina taught society about women's talents, leadership, organization, and determination.

Rose Kohler (1873–1947)

The first Jewish settlers came to the United States as early as the mid-seventeenth century. It was not until the nineteenth century, however, that Jews arrived in large numbers as persecution in Eastern Europe forced them to seek a new home in America. In their native villages, Jews were largely segregated in closed com-munities called *shtetls*. Yet upon arriving in the United

States, Jewish immigrants found themselves facing problems of integration and assimilation as they sought to preserve their culture while living among peoples of other customs and faiths.

Especially in this new environment, women played a crucial role in passing on Jewish traditions. The woman dressed the children, prepared the house, and cooked the meal for *Shabbat*, the Sabbath or day of rest. Girls were raised to become good Jewish wives and mothers who had many obligations for the survival of the faith. Nevertheless, their roles and rights were limited compared to those of men. For example, a woman was not counted in the *minyan*, the required number of at least ten people needed for public prayer. Regardless of her religious devotion, a Jewish woman was not considered a full member of the congregation, nor did she have voting privileges in the congregation. Rose Kohler spoke out against these injustices.

Rose came from a prominent Jewish family; both her father and her grandfather were Reform rabbis. She became a noted artist, specializing in painting and sculpting. Rose took an active role in the Reform movement and became chairperson of the Committee on Religious Schools of the National Council of Jewish Women. Out of her concern for education, Rose recognized the contradiction in teaching Jewish boys and girls about their religious heritage but then preventing girls from going beyond a certain point in their education. In 1895, Rose delivered a speech before the National Council arguing that this was unfair. She asked why boys and girls grew up to have different Jewish obligations when they were treated as equals as children.

The contradiction that Rose raised was a concern of many Jewish women and men. Rose, and Jews like her, dared to raise important questions about her tradition and changes that she believed would improve Judaism.

19

She helped to pave the way for a change that took place twenty-five years after her death, when the first woman in the United States was ordained a rabbi.

Dorothy Day (1897–1980)

Dorothy Day learned about poverty at an early age. She was born in Brooklyn, New York, the third of five children. Her family moved to Oakland, California, when she was a girl, but their home was destroyed by an earthquake. The Day family then settled on Chicago's West Side, where they struggled to make the best of what they had left. Dorothy saw many poor people around her in the Chicago slums and realized the injustice of some people's having so much while others had so little. She later devoted her life to challenging and correcting these abuses.

At sixteen Dorothy entered the University of Illinois at Urbana, to which she had received a scholarship. But after two years of study, she dropped out, eager to work in ways that would further her commitment to help others. She moved to New York and got a job with a socialist newspaper. There she became involved in supporting workers and their rights. During the next few years, Dorothy lived in different places and worked at various jobs while writing and traveling. Finally she settled in an artists' colony in Staten Island, New York, where she met Forster Battingham, who became her common-law husband. In 1927, Dorothy gave birth to their daughter, Tamar Teresa. She had her baby baptized and joined the Roman Catholic Church.

By then the Great Depression was strangling the nation. While managing to find enough work to get by, Dorothy was affected by the hunger and poverty that surrounded her. She felt strongly that the Church needed to be true to its call and help people in their daily lives. Toward this goal, she and a newfound friend and colleague, Peter Maurin, founded a newspaper, the *Catholic Worker*. As the first issues were distributed in 1933, Dorothy and Peter, without realizing it, were launching one of the most important organizations of the Depression.

The *Catholic Worker* espoused a fierce commitment to social justice. The paper concentrated on upholding the rights of workers while advocating racial equality and opposing anti-Semitism. Soon a movement grew around the paper and its founders, as Dorothy and Peter began providing services that embodied their commitment. They opened "houses of hospitality," first in New York and then nationwide, offering food and shelter to people in need. Hundreds would line up at their doors for bread, coffee, and soup. Volunteers, many of whom were women, moved into these houses to help out. Peter and Dorothy also organized groups of scholars, workers, priests, and students to meet and share their ideas. These forums soon were taking place across the country. What started as one woman's commitment to social justice eventually grew into a national movement.

Until her death in 1980, Dorothy Day remained a vocal proponent of justice for all people. In the 1950s and '60s she was active in the civil rights movement, even when this meant risking her life by taking a stand against racists. She became an advocate for migrant workers' rights in the 1970s, protesting unsafe labor conditions and unfair wages. In her seventies, Dorothy remained true to the causes she believed in, even when the consequences of her actions landed her in jail. In a prayer that she wrote after just getting out of jail in 1973, Dorothy appealed to the Pope and her readers to help make the world a place where justice flourishes.

The life of Dorothy Day shows the impact that one committed woman can make, even without a position of power or prestige in her religious community. Her writings, her work, her life-style, and her faith show that she was a woman of great integrity. Dorothy Day responded wholeheartedly to the mandate of her faith to love God and others and to create justice.

Bishop Barbara Harris (1930–)

Barbara Harris was born in Philadelphia into a third-generation Episcopal family. When she was twelve years old, she heard a sermon about racism in the church and realized how unfair it was that blacks were not bishops in her church, and women were not permitted to become ministers. Little did she realize that she, a black girl, would become the first woman bishop of the Episcopal Church.

To many people, Barbara Harris was an unlikely choice for the position of bishop because she had not followed the traditional route to such a role of authority. Throughout much of her life, she lived her faith and devotion to her church without holding any official position or title. In the 1960s she became active in the civil rights movement, and she joined in the historic march, with Dr. Martin Luther King Jr., from Selma to Birmingham, Alabama. One summer Barbara took her vacation from her job as a public relations executive for an oil company to go to Greenville, Mississippi, and help register blacks to vote. She volunteered as a lay chaplain for prisoners. Through these experiences and her involvement in her church, Barbara felt a growing call to be ordained.

In the late 1970s, ordination to the priesthood was an altogether new option for Episcopal women. In 1974 at Barbara's church in Philadelphia, the Church of the Advocate, a service was held to ordain the first eleven women priests in the Episcopal Church, even though their ordination was unauthorized. Barbara Harris participated in this milestone service, but not as one of the

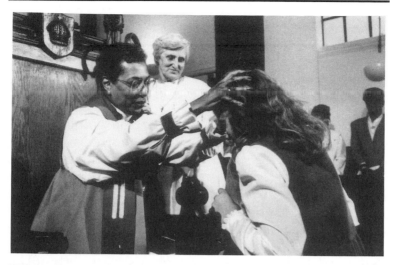

Bishop Barbara Harris, the first woman bishop in the Episcopal Church, confirms a church member (photo by James Solheim; courtesy of Episcopal News Service).

women ordained. She served as the crucifer, carrying the cross in the processional. In retrospect, this action foreshadowed the role Barbara would later take, leading priests, introducing opportunities for women, and changing the church, when she became a bishop.

Barbara was ordained a deacon in 1979 and a priest in 1980. She acquired her theological training through an alternative educational program of the Diocese of Pennsylvania, and took courses at Metropolitan Collegiate Center in Philadelphia as well as at Villanova University. Studying at night, on weekends, and during vacations, she took the same ordination exams given to seminarians, passed with flying colors, and was ordained. Her first position as a priest was at St. Augustine of Hippo Church in Philadelphia; at the same time she served as a chaplain at the Philadelphia County Prison. In 1984 she became executive director of the Episcopal

Church Publishing Company. She also worked as editor, columnist, and publisher for the Episcopal journal *The Witness*. Through her writings, Barbara was quickly recognized as a forceful voice for prisoners' rights, justice for lesbians and gays, and racial equality.

It was her reputation as an advocate of social justice that helped gain support for Barbara's nomination as bishop. Because of her background and her unconventional journey to the priesthood, not to mention her sex and her race, the choice of Barbara Harris as a bishop was highly controversial. Some Episcopal clergymen were still opposed to women as priests, let alone bishops, and saw her nomination as a source of divisiveness in the Church. Others complained that her credentials were shaky and her experience was limited. Still others did not like her political and theological views, which they considered "radical." Commenting on these criticisms, Barbara quipped, "I could be a combination of the Virgin Mary, Lena Horne, and Madame Curie, and I would still get clobbered by some." In September 1988, after several close ballots for the suffragan (assistant) bishop of the Diocese of Massachusetts, Barbara Harris did become bishop.

In her first sermon after election, Barbara told her congregation, "A fresh wind is indeed blowing across the church. Things thought to be impossible just a short time ago are coming to be." She added, "For some, these changes are refreshing breezes. For others, they are as fearsome as a hurricane." Bishop Barbara Harris does not want to instill fear in anyone, even though she is a powerful person in her church. As a bishop, she uses her position to work for human rights for all people. She states her goals simply: "I am talking about moving into the mainstream of those who seek God's justice, of those who seek God's peace, of those who seek God's brotherhood and sisterhood."

Rabbi Sally Priesand (1946–   )

When Sally Priesand was growing up in Cleveland, there were no women rabbis in the United States. Across the Atlantic, a German woman, Regina Jonas, had received a Hebrew rabbinical diploma and had functioned briefly as a rabbi in the late thirties, but she was thrown into a concentration camp in 1940 and died there. As a girl, Sally did not know about Regina Jonas or that there had ever been a woman rabbi. But from high school on, she knew that this was what she wanted to do with her life.

For decades before Sally's ordination, the question of women in the rabbinate had been debated. Tradition, more than any formal doctrine or rule, had barred women. Jewish teachings hold that each person has equal dignity and worth; however, women and men were understood to have separate roles and responsibilities. The household, not the spiritual leadership of the synagogue, was considered the realm of a woman. Nonetheless some women felt compelled to become rabbis. In the early 1920s, Martha Neumark, a student at the Reform rabbinical school of Hebrew Union College, put the question before the faculty when she asked permission to lead High Holy Day services. After much discussion, the Board of Governors ruled that the time was not right and no change should be made in the practice of limiting admission to the rabbinate to men. This sentiment was reiterated in 1939 when Helen Hadassah Levinthal completed the rabbinical course of studies at the Jewish Institute of Religion and sought ordination. In 1956 a committee of the Central Conference of American Rabbis was formed to examine the issue; this time they approved of women becoming rabbis. Yet it was not until Sally Priesand's ordination in 1972 that a Jewish woman in the United States actually entered the rabbinate.

When Sally began her studies at the Cincinnati branch of the Hebrew Union College–Jewish Institute of Religion, she was not intending to break ground for generations to come. She simply knew that she wanted to be a rabbi. At first some of the faculty mistakenly assumed that Sally had come to seminary to find a husband, but she eventually won their respect. By her sixth year of school, it was clear that she would become the first woman rabbi in this country. As a "first," she was expected to give interviews, make appearances, and deliver statements on contemporary issues. Sally remembers, "Surprisingly enough, though I have always considered myself an introvert, I somehow managed to cope with these new pressures." After eight years of rabbinical study, Sally Priesand was ordained on June 3, 1972. Her classmates rose to their feet in an ovation, and Sally wept with joy. A new era in Judaism had begun.

But many challenges remained. Once she was ordained, Sally needed to find a position, and some synagogues refused even to interview her. However, the Stephen Wise Free Synagogue in New York was glad to have Rabbi Sally Priesand join its staff as assistant rabbi. In helping to lead this congregation, Sally preached, conducted worship services, taught members of all ages, attended committee meetings, supervised the youth program, counseled, and officiated at life-cycle events such as weddings, baby-namings, and funerals. She also was in demand to lecture around the country, as her very presence introduced the reality of women rabbis.

Soon women began to enter the rabbinate in increasing numbers. The Reconstructionist Rabbinical College, established in 1968, encouraged the ordination of women from its beginning. In 1974, Sandy Eisenberg Sasso became the first woman ordained as a Recon-

Rabbi Sally Priesand, the first woman ordained a rabbi in the United States, chants the prayers for the service of the Torah scroll (photo courtesy Rabbi Sally Priesand).

structionist rabbi. In the Conservative movement, the debate about ordaining women focused on discussion of whether or not such an action was *halakhic* (in accordance with Jewish law). After years of study,

27

a commission of faculty at the Conservative Jewish Theological Seminary of America voted to accept women as rabbinical candidates. Amy Eilberg became the first woman Conservative rabbi; she was ordained in 1985. Today nearly half of all candidates for the rabbinate in these movements are women.

Still a devoted congregational leader, Sally cherishes the sense of community that her work offers. Her days are busy fulfilling the duties of a rabbi, while teaching people about the richness of Jewish heritage. Despite the difficulties and prejudices that she encountered, Sally finds being a rabbi enormously satisfying. She encourages others to pursue a life's work that they too will find energizing and meaningful. By their accomplishments, she believes, clergywomen will gain respect, which in turn leads to acceptance. Rabbi Sally Priesand urges, "Women must now take the initiative."

And You?

Over the centuries, many women have taken the initiative, gained respect, and prepared the way for women to pursue careers as clergy. The ordination of women in mainline Protestant churches and in the Reform, Reconstructionist, and Conservative branches of Judaism is a collective accomplishment of many people, most of whose names we will never know. The women discussed in these pages held fast to their convictions, usually despite great pressure from society to limit their roles and opportunities. Their courageous struggle succeeded in expanding the possibilities for women. As we venture into the next millennium, we need to recognize the powerful witness of those who have enabled us to come this far.

But there is still a long way to go. Not all women who feel called to ordination have the option available in their religion. And women who are ordained still face obstacles to acceptance and recognition. The pioneering days for clergywomen are far from over; many congregations have yet to experience their first woman rabbi or minister. As clergy, women are not trying to become "honorary men" and follow exactly in the ways of their forefathers. Rather, in charting new courses, women open up fresh possibilities for ministry while looking to each other as role models. Clergywomen are shaping communities of faith that are vital and relevant to our modern world with its unique challenges.

As they face the future, many synagogues and churches may look to young women like you. Is a career as a clergywoman the path that you want your life to take? For some women today, as in years past, the decision to become a minister or rabbi comes with strong inner determination. For others, active involvement in their religious tradition naturally leads them to consider ordination. As you discover more about becoming a clergywoman, remember the variety of experiences and backgrounds that women have brought to these vocations. New possibilities for women in religion continue to unfold. Sisters who paved the way invite you to join them today in moving toward an exciting future.

3

Steps to Take: Becoming a Clergywoman

Among the stimulating questions that a person considering a career as a clergywoman might ask herself are, "Am I called to this work?" "Is this what God wants me to do with my life?" "How do I know if this is right for me?" Along with the practical career considerations, the decision of whether or not to become a clergywoman carries a deep spiritual dimension. Christians tend to speak of it as their "call" to ordained ministry, generally referring to an inner assurance, experience, sign, or vision that this is what they are meant to do. A call may be as dramatic as a voice or an image that takes its recipient by surprise, or it can be as subtle as a gentle, growing understanding that fills her with a strong sense that she should be ordained. Jews rarely use the word "call," but instead may refer to a passion for Judaism that led them to study for the rabbinate. For many rabbis and ministers, a love of their tradition and belief in God lead them to consider a career as clergy. But the spiritual questions and experiences involved in making the decision vary widely.

For some, the thought of becoming a minister or rabbi enters their mind and heart and then gradually takes hold in their life. Some clergywomen come from a religious background; others report that religion was never important in their home. Quite a few women recall that the thought of becoming a clergywoman arose during their junior high and high school years. They then went on to explore whether the career would be right for them, just as you are doing now. One minister explains the process of reaching her decision this way:

> I heard my call to ministry when I was twelve. While I was not raised in a religious home, my mother felt that providing me with a religious education was part of her parental responsibilities, so I attended Sunday school since I was four. I loved it and looked forward to it each week! The Bible stories were so exciting, as I read about people, ordinary people like me, through whom God worked out God's purpose. Church music became an important way that I learned about God, and I became part of the children's choir at age eight. As the years went by, the church and the role of faith became more and more central to my life. At twelve our music minister asked me if I had ever thought about becoming a minister when I grew up. I hadn't, but he planted a seed that quickly took root—of course, this was what I was to do with my life! The more I thought about it, prayed about it, talked about it, the more sure I became of this call.

As in this account, a number of women describe having a personal knowledge or desire that this is what they should do, and through involvement in church and synagogue activities their feelings are confirmed.

Sometimes a call is much more sudden, when a specific incident invites and excites a person to serve

God with her life. One pastor says her call was just such a moment:

> I was on a retreat. After two days of fasting and prayer, I received my call. I saw an image of myself covered in light and there was also an image of Christ saying, "I want you to preach my Gospel and lead my people." The image kept recurring. The next day the leader of the retreat said that God had told her to pray for two people who were called. Another woman was called to teach and I was called to preach. We had both received visions.

One minister describes a life-changing experience that influenced her:

> My call came from my illness when I was thirteen years old. I was sick and later diagnosed as having leukemia. I stopped breathing and had a tracheotomy, but I was still in critical condition. I was dying, and the members of my home church held a prayer meeting every night. God saved me and gave me life. Even though I was young, I knew that in the future I would serve God in some way. I had been told that I was going to live six months to a year. That was fourteen years ago.

These descriptions show how intense the calls can be that prompt some women to seek ordination.

Many clergywomen come to the awareness of their vocation far more gradually, as professional and spiritual considerations seem to come together naturally. One clergywoman describes becoming a rabbi as a fulfillment of the work she enjoys:

Being a rabbi brings together a lot of things that I love very much. In this profession I can do everything that is important to me: write, preach, study, teach, paint, sing, learn, listen, counsel, help. As I was considering what I should do with my life, I realized that there are a lot of things that I love, but only one thing that I am passionate about: my Judaism.

Two ministers remember similar feelings:

My call was rather subtle. When deciding what career to pursue I considered social work, teaching, counseling, and other people-oriented fields, but I found my interest in people was closely related to my faith in God and I couldn't separate the two. I also liked the "renaissance" quality of the ministry.

I wanted to combine my growing love for Christ with my theater background. I wanted to apply my faith to my love of the arts. I never dreamed of being ordained—but here I am! God certainly has a sense of humor (as well as lots of love)!

The opportunity to combine so much of yourself and what you love attracts many women to consider careers as clergy.

Years ago, women who felt called to become rabbis and ministers were prohibited from being ordained. Even when women first began to be ordained, women clergy were much rarer than they are today. A minister explains, "People sometimes ask me if I always wanted to be a minister. When I was growing up, I never *met* a woman who was a minister. I saw my first clergywoman when I was in seminary." Often women who dared to

Rev. Karen Sapio, a Presbyterian pastor, is a youth minister.

acknowledge their conviction to become clergy were not quite sure what they would end up doing with their lives. One woman tells how she first interpreted her own desire to *become* a minister as a yearning to *marry* a minister.

I was called as a young child, but because I'd never seen any women ministers I thought that this meant I wanted to marry a minister. As I grew up I committed my life to Christian service and church camp and wanted to be a Director of Christian Education or a missionary (places where I saw women in ministry). Then my husband began seminary and I saw women in ministry and said, "God, is this what you want me to do?" and the Spirit and the Church said, "Yes!"

A rabbi aslo recalls the challenge of considering a career as clergy when she had no women as role models:

> It is not possible to put my finger on exactly what moved me to make such a decision. It was a combination of challenging ideas, compelling and caring people, words of faith, and the poetry of the soul. My own rabbi encouraged me and helped to shape my vision of the rabbinate. I was sixteen when I first considered becoming a rabbi. At that time no woman had been ordained as a rabbi.

Because ordained women are still a minority among clergy, it is important to find people who are supportive of you and your interest. One clergywoman relates her pastor's response when she told him she was thinking of becoming a minister:

> I went to my pastor and said, "I think I feel called to the ministry." He asked if my call was in an appropriate field [for women] such as youth work, missions, or Christian education. When I said that I felt called to the ordained ministry, he told me to wait and see if it passes.

Fortunately, she ignored his advice. The encouragement that another minister received seems more common:

> My call certainly was not a voice from on high . . . ministry seemed to be the only vocation that encompassed the things most important to me— working with people, teaching, learning myself, and spiritual growth and searching. I received a lot of affirmation from my pastor and other people around me when I made my first noises about "maybe . . . going to seminary . . ."

Affirmation is a crucial part of a clergywoman's decision to enter the ministry.

At the same time, it is important to recognize the difference between encouragement and pressure. Are you interested in a career as a clergywoman yourself, or are you motivated by someone else's expectations? Maybe your minister or rabbi would like to see you carry on in his or her footsteps. Maybe you have relatives who are clergy, and you are looked to as the one who will continue the tradition. For others to suggest this career might be helpful, but for them to put a strain on you would be unfair. If this vocation is not attractive to you, you probably would not enjoy the work or do it well. Listen to your inner feelings.

Personally and spiritually, what leads you to consider becoming a clergywoman is a unique part of who you are. Your call might be a dramatic vision with a voice from on high, or it might be a career decision filled with voices from around you. Your motivation might come from a sense of gratitude to God for a miracle in your life or a profound appreciation of your religious tradition. The possibilities are limitless. When born of soul-searching reflection, no one way to sense this call or compulsion is any more or less valid than any other. Revelatory visions are not "ridiculous" or "hallucinogenic," and eventual decisions are not "feeble" or "unauthentic." Each woman's way of recognizing and claiming the desire to serve God through the ministry is as special as she is herself.

As you consider becoming a clergywoman, you need to be honest with yourself. Think about these questions:

- How do I feel when I picture myself, years from now, as a clergywoman?
- Does this call or desire come from my own inner

self, or is it an expectation that others have placed upon me?
- How do I sense God's role in this process?
- Why does this career seem right for me?

Those are big questions, but there is no need to have the answers right away. By keeping your mind, spirit, and heart open and truthful, you can be sure that you will proceed with integrity.

PERSONALLY AND PRACTICALLY, IS THIS FOR ME?

A lot of what a clergywoman does is related to who she is, since the vocation asks you to pour yourself into your daily work. As you think about becoming a minister or rabbi, you will discover that certain talents, traits, skills, and abilities can help you. Here are some characteristics that would be an asset to you as a clergywoman. They can also serve as guidelines as you explore whether you are well suited for the career and the career is well suited for you.

DO I HAVE...?

1. A love of God/A strong faith

A clergywoman believes in God and loves God. Commitment to God and her faith are central to her life. She leads others in prayers and devotions that are meaningful to her as well. As one clergywoman asserts, "You need to have a deep, close, life-giving friendship with God." At the same time, a clergywoman often wrestles with how God works through each day. If you are a clergywoman, you are not an atheist, viewing the horrors of humanity and then declaring that God does not exist. Nor are you hopelessly naive or unwaveringly cynical. You see pain and misery, as well as joy and promise, and you explore how God works through it all.

37

In the Reform, Reconstructionist, and Conservative movements of Judaism, the vast majority of rabbis believe in God. It is possible, however, to be an agnostic —one who has no absolute belief in God—and still be a rabbi. Such a person realizes that the Divinity cannot be defined and asks intellectual, spiritual, and religious questions about God's existence. Yet her questioning takes place within the framework of Jewish belief and in the tradition of Jewish philosophy. She may be convinced of some greater power that inspires strong faith and yet classify herself as an agnostic as she refuses to define God.

The serious inquirer who is deeply tied to her Jewish or Christian tradition, but is developing her understanding of God, may become an especially valuable rabbi or minister because she can understand the doubts of others. No one, and certainly not a clergyperson, should pretend to have all the answers about God; anyone who feels that she knows everything there is to know about God only parades her arrogance and ignorance. Instead, a clergywoman asks questions while believing that there is indeed a power of love far greater than she can comprehend.

2. A love of people
Do you honestly like people? A clergywoman's days are often filled with interaction with others. Because of her position in the community, she is sought for the help, enthusiasm, wisdom, guidance, support, ideas, and counsel that she can offer. Since meeting with so many people can be very demanding, one clergywoman gives this advice: "Be sure that you genuinely love people; otherwise you will be easily defeated and frustrated." If you honestly enjoy being with people, you may find that work as a clergywoman is highly energizing.

3. A genuine desire to help others

Are you willing, even eager, to help others? A clergy-woman must try to understand those who come to her seeking comfort or counsel. People going through difficulties often turn first to their minister or rabbi as someone they already know and trust. A clergywoman values that precious trust. That is not the same as immediately having the right answers or the perfect solutions. Rather, a clergywoman might listen to what the person is going through and perhaps offer a prayer, hold a hand, or enable the person to get additional help.

A clergywoman also looks toward the local and global communities, envisioning ways to improve life for all people. She believes that painful situations in the world can improve, but only if people like her are part of them. For example, a rabbi might exert her efforts toward helping Russian Jews settle in Israel, although she may never meet these Russian Jews herself. A pastor might encourage her congregation to adopt a "sister church" in Latin America, initiating a long-term relationship of increased international understanding. Through her role and religious affiliation, a clergy-woman has access to avenues of help beyond her immediate surroundings.

4. A love of my faith tradition

An aspiring clergywoman is usually part of a community of faith. While growing up, she may have gone to worship each week, although that is not the experience of every clergywoman. Most clergy tend to be ordained in the tradition of their families, but again that is not always the case. If you decide to seek ordination, one of your first steps—if you have not already done so—is to find a congregation, denomination, or movement where you will be nurtured and supported.

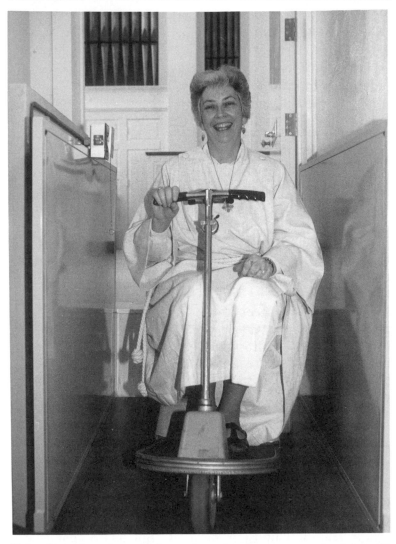

Helen Betenbaugh, an Episcopal seminarian, uses a wheelchair lift to enter the chapel and preach at the Perkins School of Theology (photo by Doug Hopfer).

Deciding which religious tradition is best for you may be easy. When you go to synagogue or church, do you find the services stimulating and moving? Does some aspect of the worship, whether it be the music, readings, or rituals, speak to your soul? Do you want to be identified with this community of faith? If this association would be a source of silent pride, you would probably represent your tradition well, as long as you respect the beliefs and practices of other religions. If you love your faith tradition, you may want to help shape its future.

Some Helpful Traits and Skills

1. Self-confidence
Self-confidence is crucial for success as a clergywoman. While believing in God, you need to believe in yourself as a person created in God's image and doing God's work. A clergywoman realizes that she is called to enter the ministry and that she has gifts, skills, and training to offer. If her ideas and opinions are to be valued by others, she must first value them herself. She listens to various points of view with an open mind, but also holds on to her own convictions. Without feeling threatened, a clergywoman must have the confidence to stand up for herself and others.

This is especially true for women. Many people have different expectations of a minister or a rabbi depending on his or her gender. People have an image of what an ideal clergyperson looks like, and seldom is that image female. A clergywoman may undertake a position to discover that some people are waiting to see if she "can handle the job," as if assuming that she will fail. Conversely, a clergywoman may be expected to be exceptionally capable because "If it's a woman doing this, she's got to be *really* good." Rarely is a clergyman scrutinized in the same way. Because such discrimination exists, a clergywoman who has healthy self-confidence knows deep down that she is helping others and serving God.

2. Leadership Ability

Can you generate enthusiasm? Do you listen well? Do you offer valuable suggestions? Can you get others to see your point of view? Do you like initiating projects and programs? Do you throw your energy into your commitments? If so, you already have leadership ability.

A clergywoman needs to embrace the responsibility of leadership. For many women that is a real challenge because they have known few women in strong roles of public leadership and so are following an uncharted course. Also women are often raised from an early age (without even realizing it) to defer to men. Society's models of leaders in government, business, and other positions of power reinforce the notion of men as "natural" leaders. As a result, people generally are not used to looking to women for leadership. One minister in her late twenties observes, "Many older parishioners see me as a niece or a granddaughter, rather than a pastor. You need to be prepared to prove yourself."

A clergywoman proves herself as she fulfills her role. She expresses her opinion and is prepared to explain it. She is forthright, but considerate. A clergywoman who tries to please everyone will quickly find herself discouraged. As one clergywoman advises, "Don't try to be everything to everyone. Just be a fair leader."

3. Social Personality

A rabbi or minister finds herself in a very social role because her work is centered on people. She engages others in the life of her faith community, as well as inviting their involvement on local, regional, and perhaps even national and international levels. People seek her presence, and she seeks theirs. However, a clergyperson need not be an extrovert who is energized by constant interaction; some clergy are more introverted. A reflective clergyperson might bring a calming influence to a hectic situation. As long as you like people, your personality can be an asset to you as a clergywoman.

4. Communication Skills

Listening well. To communicate capably, a clergyperson first needs to listen well. In some circumstances, such as a counseling session, the importance of hearing another's concerns are obvious. A rabbi or minister also uses her listening skills as she learns of a person's needs or the community's problems through casual conversation. Good listening is an especially valuable skill when a clergywoman's responsibilities involve regular preaching. Once a clergyperson can listen well, she can speak effectively to the individuals and community she serves.

Speaking well. A clergywoman is often called upon to speak, both privately and publicly. Privately she may meet with someone who is very upset, and her words can be comforting. Publicly she is called on to preach, teach, and speak both to her community of faith and beyond. She is prepared to address issues around her work and to speak up on behalf of those she serves. A clergywoman is frequently called upon to offer prayers, invocations, benedictions, and blessings at private celebrations and public functions. Public speaking is part of her role as an ordained person, and she responds professionally.

Writing well. Before a minister's or rabbi's words are spoken, they are often written down. How much written preparation one does before speaking varies greatly among religious traditions, as well as among

43

individuals. Whether or not a clergyperson chooses to have a prayer, sermon, or speech prepared word for word, she needs to write to fulfill her responsibilities. She may write letters, newsletters, articles, reports, and various other documents in the course of her work. As a leader in the community, she may contribute to newspapers or magazines or write more extensive publications. Since we live in a highly verbal society, a successful clergyperson needs to know how to use both the spoken and written word effectively.

5. Organizational Ability

Because the work of a rabbi or minister is varied and demanding, a clergyperson needs to be organized. Few occupations for clergy consist only of contact with people. Most involve administrative duties such as handling budgets, finances, and reports and the general management of the organization that makes service and outreach possible. Part of organizational ability is the skill of networking and discovering who can offer the right assistance. Structures of the denominations or movements also may provide guidance and resources. A clergyperson who takes on all responsibilities herself may end up feeling like a "lone ranger" (and an exhausted one!). A clergyperson who is organized and knows what needs to be done can delegate tasks and mobilize others to help accomplish the desired goals.

6. Self-Motivation

A minister or rabbi determines much of her schedule herself. While she has obligations and requirements that she must fulfill, her days still allow for flexibility. Someone who likes to be told what to do each moment may spend too much time wondering what to do next. A motivated clergywoman sees what needs to be done and sets out to do it, by herself or by enlisting the help of others.

7. Patience

A rabbi or minister needs to be patient as she works her way into the life of the community. Her idealism about what she would like to accomplish must be combined with a realistic understanding of what is feasible. She realizes that, even in the best of circumstances, change takes time, and she expects gradual instead of instant improvement.

For women who are clergy, there is another dimension to the patience required: patience with those who object to you because you are an ordained woman. A cantor describes what it was like when she began working at her temple and many in the congregation were upset that a man was not chosen for the position. "People say they were not happy at first," she explains, "but they don't feel that way anymore. You just have to hang in there and hope that they come around." That is not to say that a clergywoman should tolerate abuse because of her gender. Rather she should proceed with her work as best she can and know that in time many of those who have expressed skepticism or even hostility will come to accept her.

8. Sense of Humor

In a profession that is so filled with life-and-death issues, a sense of humor is crucial. Since a rabbi's or minister's days can be intense, the ability to laugh, even at herself, is bound to serve her well. Humor also helps a clergywoman distinguish between problems that demand great attention and those that do not.

Without a sense of humor, a clergywoman runs the risk of becoming angry or callous or discouraged all too quickly. Since a clergywoman is still likely to encounter discrimination, she needs to be prepared to defend herself. An effective way to do that is with humor. A woman who is an Episcopal rector smiles when members of her congregation introduce her as, ". . . the Father . . . my Mother . . . the priest." One young minister recalls being approached at a party by a man who said, "So I understand that you are a *lady* minister." "Yes," she acknowledged, "and I hear that you are a *gentleman* dentist." Humor invites people to a see a situation from a new perspective.

9. A Realistic Sense of Self

A clergyperson is motivated, is patient, has a sense of humor, and pours her energy, skills, learning, heart and soul into her life's work; at the same time she knows that she will make mistakes. A sense of her strengths and limitations is essential as she manages her work while paying attention to her personal life. She does not try to fulfill all expectations, realizing that the ability to be everywhere at the same time belongs only to God. Instead she finds and uses the resources and support available. An enthusiastic and enduring clergywoman is optimistic and idealistic, but also realistic.

Perhaps one day you will become a clergywoman. Determining whether this should be your career is an ongoing process of reflecting, questioning, praying, studying, analyzing, growing, and wondering both privately and with others. This outline of characteristics is intended to provide you with some tools to help you make the decision. If these personal qualities seem to describe you and your abilities, you already have a head start as you advance on this career path.

EDUCATION

As an educated member of society, a clergywoman is expected to be knowledgeable. She has studied the Scriptures, knows her religious tradition, and is ready to communicate her ideas. She is a leader in her community and is reasonably well informed about local and global issues. That does not mean that a clergywoman has to be a born genius or have all the answers. Rather, she likes to learn about a wide variety of subjects and to exchange ideas with others. Her mind is open to fresh insights while she develops and maintains her own convictions. To acquire information and learning skills that she will use throughout her life, a clergywoman first obtains a solid education.

The degree of formal schooling required to become a clergywoman varies among faith traditions. In many of the more conservative churches, qualifications for ordination depend less on academic preparation and more on a spiritual call. Some denominations offer flexible programs of independent study. In most mainline Protestant denominations, an ordination candidate usually obtains her four-year college degree and then proceeds to graduate study for a Master of Divinity (M.Div.) degree, which generally takes three years of full-time study. In Jewish tradition, the rabbi is considered a teacher and therefore needs to be well educated in the Scriptures and the history of Judaism. Before being ordained, a student completes a rabbinical course of study of approximately five years in addition to college. As part of her education, the rabbinic student is awarded a Master of Arts degree. Upon completion of the program, she is ordained and receives a certificate of *semikhah* (ordination). Education is a very important step in becoming a clergywoman.

Education can also be very expensive. Many religious organizations realize this and help to support their students financially. As you and your family seek ways to pay for your education, inquire about financial resources that your church or synagogue may offer. Is there a scholarship fund in your congregation? Does some group, perhaps a women's organization, have funds available for future clergy? Does your minister or rabbi know of possibilities worth exploring? Some religious national offices and agencies offer low-interest loans and partial scholarships to college or seminary students. A list of some of these resources can be found in the Appendix. More funds are available locally, so be sure to investigate organizations in your community. If you are considering a career as a clergy-woman, your religious tradition may help you in many ways—spiritually, personally, and financially.

College ... and Beyond

As you look toward higher education, first you need to consider where you will pursue your undergraduate studies. In choosing a college, a high school student determines which would be the best school for her as she weighs academic, financial, geographic, and personal considerations. If you are thinking about becoming a clergywoman, your years in college can be a crucial part of your journey of faith. For example, find out if a college has a religious affiliation. Does it have a chaplaincy program? Are worship services held on campus? If not, how far off campus would you need to go to worship? The answers to these questions may help you decide on an institution.

You should also investigate whether the school offers strong courses and resources in your area of scholastic interest. As an undergraduate, you need not major in religion as a prerequisite for graduate theological study. In fact, most seminaries encourage students to obtain a broad-based liberal arts education, specializing in what interests them most. Remember that a well-rounded college education can only serve you well.

Use your time in college to acquire academic skills. Develop good study habits. Learn how to write clearly, as this skill is necessary for graduate school and the work of a rabbi or minister. Take courses in public speaking. The undergraduate years offer an opportunity to cultivate the communications skills that are essential to the people-centered work of a clergyperson.

Because a clergyperson comes into contact with people of many backgrounds, knowledge of a foreign language can be very helpful. In our increasingly multicultural society, the ability to speak foreign languages is more important than ever. The U.S. Census Bureau estimates that by the year 2000 fully one tenth of the population will speak Spanish as its first language. Especially if you are considering working in an urban area, a knowledge of Spanish can be a valuable asset. If you are bilingual from your own family background, you already have great skills to offer in building bridges between your community and the dominant English-speaking culture. A minister or rabbi increases her effectiveness when she can communicate in languages other than her own.

Ancient languages are part of most seminarians' education. The Bible was written in Hebrew, Aramaic, and Greek; students who know those languages can understand the scriptural text better and may even be able to translate passages for themselves. Christian seminaries generally assume that entering students have no prior knowledge of these languages, and studies begin at the introductory level. Some denominations require candidates to be familiar with biblical languages before they are ordained. Yet while in college, the future Christian seminarian does not need to concentrate on learning ancient languages.

Jewish seminaries, however, expect first-year rabbinical students to enter with a knowledge of Hebrew. Admissions officers at seminaries in the Reform, Reconstructionist, and Conservative movements urge candidates to learn as much Hebrew as possible before arriving at seminary.

Spending some time in Israel before entering seminary is also strongly recommended for a future rabbi. While one year of rabbinical study is spent in Israel, to have experienced Israel before going to seminary gives a Jew the chance to see her religion lived out in vibrant ways. It is a religious and cultural experience that is inspirational for many, because Israeli society is primarily built around Jewish life-style and customs. Also, study in Israel helps a student to learn Hebrew and become familiar with Judaica, the entire body of Jewish knowledge and literature. You might work a summer on a *kibbutz*[1] or spend a semester or a year studying at an Israeli university. Your college career provides the flexibility that could enable you to live abroad.

Many colleges either offer study programs abroad or can direct you to programs of other schools. College credit from the foreign institution can usually be applied to your home school. Financially, the cost of tuition that would be spent at your college generally can be transferred (along with any financial aid) to a program that receives your school's approval. Regardless of your religion or where you might be interested in studying abroad, be it the Middle East, Europe, Latin America, Asia, or Africa, living in a foreign country is an experience of a lifetime.

Along with cultural, social, and intellectual growth, your college years can be a time of spiritual development. Investigate the options for religious community at your school. What is the chaplaincy program like? Is there a Hillel office or campus ministry center? This can be a great way to meet other students of your faith while exploring your own religious identity. If your campus has no chaplaincy program, you might form a group of students to meet around holidays, undertake service

---

[1] Israeli commune devoted to industry or agriculture.

Seminary students Susan Steinberg (left) and Pat Jones prepare for a church history examination at Vanderbilt Divinity School (photo by Sharon Reddick).

projects, or gather to pray. Your spiritual growth while you are in college can be important to you personally and professionally.

If you become involved in a chaplaincy community, you can also try out your skills as a future clergywoman. You might become a leader of the campus Hillel club or Christian fellowship group. You might preach in a campus service. You could work with the chaplain and suggest activities. If the two of you get along well, this person might become a mentor for you and eventually help you to sort through options for your next step after graduation.

Upon completion of college, you should decide whether to proceed directly to seminary or first spend some time out of school. Both choices have advantages.

51

Students who are eager to be ordained as soon as possible will probably choose to go directly to seminary. Others prefer to work, travel, or join a volunteer program before entering graduate school. If you would like to investigate some of these opportunities, you might begin by talking with your rabbi or minister. Does she or he know of any programs, perhaps affiliated with your religion, that would appeal to you? A partial list of religious volunteer/study/work programs is given in the Appendix. Whether you enter a program, get a job, or go directly to seminary is a personal decision, but realize that many options are available.

On to Seminary

As you consider applying to seminary,[1] once again you need to investigate which institution would be best for you. You might talk with ministers or rabbis and ask them where they studied. Would they recommend the same seminary for you? Why or why not? Is this seminary affiliated with your denomination or movement? Does the school tend to be theologically conservative or progressive? What are the faculty's areas of expertise? What sorts of careers do graduates pursue?

You might also find out about the status of women at the school. Are there women on the faculty? Do they have tenured positions, or are they "visiting professors"? Will they still be there when you arrive? Are there courses that address women's concerns, such as women in ministry, or feminist theology? Is there a women's support group? What are the percentages of men and

---

[1] An institution of graduate theological learning may be called a *seminary* when it is an independent institution; a *divinity school* when it is a graduate school of a university; or a *college* as with Hebrew Union College or the Reconstructionist Rabbinical College. Since all accomplish the purpose of theological training, for convenience all are here called *seminaries*.

women in the student body? In the faculty and administration? Do women students feel fully accepted, or do they need to prove themselves more than men? For honest insights into daily life and attitudes at the seminary, talk to some women students.

As you look ahead to at least seven to nine years of combined college and graduate study, it may seem that an eternity of classes, library hours, dormitory rooms, and final exams lies before you. However, many clergywomen view their years in college and seminary as a particularly stimulating period, filled with opportunities to make lifelong friends. Most important, these years immersed in scholarship offer you a precious time to discover more about yourself, the world, and your faith.

Jewish Seminaries

For future rabbis, where you study corresponds to your movement of Judaism. Are you seeking to become a Reform, Reconstructionist, or Conservative rabbi? If you are unclear which movement is right for you, but you are still committed to studying for the rabbinate, the book *To Learn and To Teach: My Life as a Rabbi* by Rabbi Alfred Gottschalk (New York: Rosen, 1988) could be helpful in clarifying distinctions among the branches of Judaism. Each movement has a separate seminary, although some of the institutions have several campuses. For more information, write to the schools at the following addresses:

Reform
Hebrew Union College–Jewish Institute of Religion
3101 Clifton Avenue
Cincinnati, OH 45220-2488
(513) 221-1875
(*Information on all four campuses can be obtained through this address.*)

Reconstructionist
Reconstructionist Rabbinical College
Church Road and Greenwood Avenue
Wyncote, PA 19095
(215) 576-0800

Conservative
Jewish Theological Seminary of America
3080 Broadway
New York, NY 10027
(212) 678-8000

Christian Seminaries

For future ministers, the choices are not so simple,
since there are hundreds of Christian seminaries in this
country. Deciding where to go to seminary can be as
broad a decision as choosing where to go to college.
Guides to graduate schools, which can be found in your
library, may be of some assistance. A complete list of
theological seminaries in the United States (with phone
numbers) is available in the *Yearbook of American and
Canadian Churches* (Constant H. Jacquet, Jr. [ed],
Nashville: Abingdon, 1990). However, few ministers
have discovered their seminary by thumbing through
long lists of graduate schools. More often they used
their personal contacts in the religious community to
help them determine which seminary was right for
them.

As you begin considering where to go to seminary,
you will naturally bear in mind concerns about location, academics, finances, and personal needs. You
might want to attend a seminary related to your denomination, where most of the faculty and students will be
from your church. Perhaps you would prefer an interdenominational school with a broader mix of faculty

and students from varied religious traditions. Some seminarians are drawn to schools affiliated with a denomination other than their own, learning how other churches work. You might also inquire about the feeling of community that exists among the students. Are worship services held frequently? Do students or faculty lead them? Bearing these considerations in mind can help you find a seminary that will help you become the minister you want to be.

ORDINATION

An ordained minister or rabbi is recognized as a religious leader. To have been given this authority, she has fulfilled the requirements set by her tradition, and so she is noted for her qualifications, education, training, and spirituality. Ordination in Christian traditions takes place in the context of a worship service; a designated member of the clergy ordains candidates through the laying on of hands. In Jewish traditions, ordination is combined with graduation at the completion of rabbinic studies. After she is ordained, the clergyperson will be referred to as "Rabbi" or "Reverend" and is expected to uphold her faith while building up the community of believers. Above all, she is to serve God and help others.

Of course, not only ordained people take on such responsibilities. Many clergy cringe at the false distinctions made between themselves and members of their congregation, as if the minister or rabbi were "more holy" than anyone else. They seek to get away from a hierarchical model that places the minister or rabbi at the top of a pyramid of those closest to God, and instead try to create communities in which all persons are respected equally. A minister or rabbi helps others to live as faithful Christians or Jews as she does so herself.

Ordination in Judaism

The word *rabbi* means "my teacher." The Jewish people experienced a crisis of faith when their Holy Temple in Jerusalem—the second one they had built—was destroyed in the year 70 CE. The Temple and its priesthood had been central to Jewish life for hundreds of years, and as a result of its destruction, new religious leadership developed. During those times of persecution, rabbis played a vital role in passing on their faith. They acquired extensive knowledge of the *Torah*, even though doing so might jeopardize their lives. As the rabbinate grew into an institution, the rabbi was looked to as a very learned person who might also serve as a judge. He (until recently, all rabbis were men) was the best-educated person in the Jewish community and was revered for his scholarship and wisdom.

The modern rabbinate has evolved from this role while changing and adapting to our society. No longer is the rabbi the only highly educated person in the community; today a rabbi's congregation often contains other professionals who are well schooled in their own fields. From the standpoint of Jewish law, the members of the congregation are also qualified to lead the community. Many of the rites and services that a rabbi performs, such as conducting worship services or presiding at funerals, are the prerogative of any knowledgeable Jew. While it is generally the rabbi who leads these rituals, the function has evolved from the expectations of the Jewish community and not from Jewish law.

The rabbi's distinction, which is not an assumption of superiority as a Jew, is her accomplishment in religious studies. To be ordained, a rabbinic candidate has undergone years of academic preparation. She has studied the Bible, the *Midrash* (an ancient rabbinic interpretation of the Scriptures), the *Talmud* (the collection of Jewish law and tradition), theology, the Hebrew language, and

Four Conservative rabbis at the Jewish Theological Seminary of America: (left to right) Rabbi Susan Grossman, Rabbi Debra Cantor, Rabbi Nina Cardin, Rabbi Lori Forman.

Jewish history, and she has spent at least one year in Israel. She has taken courses in professional development and has been instructed in practical aspects of her work as a rabbi such as preaching, counseling, leading

57

worship, and educating. She has worked in a field placement position, which has given her experience in the rabbinate while expanding her abilities and improving her skills. Reform and Reconstructionist rabbinic candidates earn the degree of Master of Arts in Hebrew Letters. Conservative candidates are awarded a Master of Arts degree during the course of study. In all three movements, the rabbi's ordination coincides with graduation.

After being ordained, a rabbi joins the rabbinic association of her movement. For the Reform movement, this is the Central Conference of American Rabbis (CCAR). The Reconstructionist organization is the Reconstructionist Rabbinical Association (RRA). Conservative rabbis join the Rabbinic Assembly (RA). These professional organizations address rabbinic concerns as well as contemporary issues in Judaism. At the same time, they bring rabbis together as colleagues, scholars, and friends.

The associations are also part of the placement system that rabbis and congregations use to find one another. The congregations of the several movements have their own organizations: the Union of American Hebrew Congregations (Reform), the Federation of Reconstructionist Congregations and Havurot (Reconstructionist), and the United Synagogue of America (Conservative). The congregational and rabbinic organizations cooperate, along with a placement commission of each movement, to fill available positions. A rabbi may qualify for a particular placement depending on the size of the congregation and the length of her experience in the rabbinate. Interviews take place in which the needs of the congregation and the qualities of the rabbi are discussed. Both the congregation and the candidate make the final decision: The congregation decides to whom to make the offer, and the rabbi decides whether to accept the position.

Ordination in Christianity

In Christian tradition, the role of the minister has evolved from the biblical legacy of the apostles. After Jesus' death, the disciples were those who carried on his ministry. While the list of the twelve disciples is sometimes used to exclude women from religious leadership as ministers and priests, the New Testament tells about women who stayed close to Jesus throughout his life and death and first witnessed the resurrection. In the biblical account of Pentecost, when the Holy Spirit descended on Jesus' followers and instructed them to proclaim the Word of God, many women were present (Acts 1:12–14, 2:1–18). According to Peter, who quotes the prophet Joel, those at that scene are fulfilling the prediction that "your sons and your daughters shall prophesy" (Acts 2:17, Joel 2:28). Jesus' followers, both men and women, were to spread the message of Jesus while offering care and compassion in his name.

Today if a person decides that she is called to carry on the mission of Jesus through ordained ministry, she engages in two processes. One is to obtain the education necessary to fulfill her tasks as a clergywoman. This is done by obtaining the Master of Divinity (M.Div.) degree. While working toward this degree, she mainly studies the Bible, church history, and theology and gains skills in preaching, leading worship, counseling, teaching, and other aspects of church leadership. She also acquires practical experience from working in a field placement.

However, ordination does not automatically coincide with graduation. Some students pursue an M.Div. because they want to study theology, but they are undecided about ordination or have no intention of becoming a minister. In some denominations, an M.Div. is not necessary to become ordained. Ordination itself involves a separate process handled through the local church or the denomination.

To be ordained, a candidate must demonstrate her call and fulfill the ordination procedure required by her church. The exact requirements vary greatly. In some denominations, qualifications are largely focused on a candidate's call and evidence of her gifts for ministry. The individual congregation evaluates a candidate's capabilities and may then decide to ordain her for service. Most mainline denominations require extensive interviews, exams, evaluations, and statements. Ordination is conferred by a clergyperson who is a representative of the national church, such as a bishop, and takes place in a worship service.

If you are considering becoming a minister, an important early step is to talk with your pastor about your goals. He or she can give you a general idea of the necessary steps in your church. Your minister probably knows you from your participation in the congregation and will be eager to support you in your decision and guide you through the process.

Although ordination procedures differ in denominations, the following are qualifications that you might need to meet to be ordained in your church:

- Active membership in a congregation for a given period (generally at least a year)
- Recommendation from your pastor
- Meetings with the appropriate committee of your congregation
- Written and oral statements of why you feel called to ordination
- Meetings with the appropriate committee of the area jurisdiction of your church (such as the association, diocese, district, presbytery, synod)
- Autobiographical statement
- Theological statement

- Statements reflecting knowledge of your church's history, polity, and doctrine
- A supervisory process with a clergyperson of your denomination
- A physical examination
- A psychological examination
- A year of full-time internship
- Transcripts from undergraduate and graduate school
- Master of Divinity degree
- Seminary faculty evaluations
- At least a year at a denominational seminary
- A retreat consisting of a series of interviews
- Interviews with the clergy of your church's jurisdictional body
- Bible examinations
- Ordination examinations (covering such topics as theology, worship, contemporary issues, church history, Bible)
- Interview with the ordaining clergyperson of your church

As you proceed toward ordination, you reach different stages of eligibility and may be successively identified as a candidate, deacon, inquirer, postulant, or student in-care, depending on your denomination.

The list of requirements may seem long and perhaps a bit intimidating, but not all the steps may be required, depending on your church. The progression is completed over the course of years, often while in seminary. Also you would not be alone, but guided by clergy and often accompanied by others undergoing the same process.

Although not everyone who feels called to ordination is assured of achieving the goal, the ordination procedure is not planned to be fiercely competitive. Still, it can be demanding, and your persistence and flexibility may decide whether you become ordained or not. Could you wait a year longer than you had planned before being ordained? Would you be willing to move to another region of the country to increase your chances of serving as a minister? The ordination process is designed to help insure that those who are ordained are not only called to the ministry, but also are capable of its challenges.

In some denominations, such as the American Baptist Church, the Episcopal Church, the Evangelical Lutheran Church in America, the Presbyterian Church (USA), and the United Church of Christ, a candidate who has completed the necessary steps is not ordained until she receives her first call, or ministerial placement. This placement is usually as a pastor in a church. Most of the denominations have clearinghouses that list available positions either nationally or regionally. A candidate submits a portfolio, often including a résumé, a personal profile, and a sample sermon. Then she is informed of congregations that are seeking a pastor and have needs that correspond to her abilities. She can also apply for positions on her own. Congregations and candidates who are interested in each other proceed to interviews and a selection process. When the candidate receives her first call, the church where she will serve as pastor often hosts a special worship service for her ordination.

In other denominations, such as the Christian Church (Disciples of Christ) and the United Methodist Church, ministers can be ordained when they have fulfilled the requirements of their tradition and before obtaining their first church position. Disciples of Christ congregations act independently and ordain those whom they find are called to ministry. In the United Methodist Church, candidates are ordained by their bishop, who subsequently appoints them to a pastoral position. Ministers in the Evangelical Lutheran Church in America are also assigned to a placement by their bishop. The bishop works in consultation with the clergy and the congregations, taking into consideration the personal and professional concerns of the minister as well as the needs of the congegation. This system helps to assure the minister a pastoral placement, and she generally accepts the position that is offered to her.

Some women discover while working toward ordination or seeking a pastoral position that it is harder for them than for their male colleagues. They may feel that they are treated unfairly by a male-dominated religious establishment. Since parts of the ordination and placement processes are based on subjective evaluations, such as interviews, it is important for a candidate or clergywoman first to determine why she is being held back or discouraged. If this should happen to you and you conclude that the reason is indeed gender discrimination, you need to proceed strategically. Most important, find allies and support. Organize with other women who have had similar experiences. Enlist the help of colleagues, both male and female, who are in positions to help you. Gather support from laity who would speak on your behalf. Realize that the days of pioneering for clergywomen are far from over, and that you are making a valuable contribution yourself.

Many clergywomen have helped to pave the way for you, as more and more women are being ordained. The following offices can help you find out your denomination's ordination requirements and answer other questions that you might have about clergywomen in your church.

Denominational Offices for Ordination Information

African Methodist Episcopal (AME) Zion
  AME Zion Church
  Office of the General Secretary
  PO Box 32843
  Charlotte, NC 28232
  (704) 332-3851

American Baptist
  Commission on the Ministry
  American Baptist Churches USA
  PO Box 851
  Valley Forge, PA 19482-0851
  (215) 768-2000

Christian Church (Disciples of Christ)
  Center for Leadership and Ministry
  Christian Church (Disciples of Christ)
  PO Box 1986
  Indianapolis, IN 46206
  (317) 353-1491

Episcopal
  Women in Mission and Ministry
  or Office of the Board for Theological Education
  Episcopal Church Center
  815 Second Avenue
  New York, NY 10017
  (800) 334-7626 (outside NY state)
  (800) 321-2231 (in NY state)

Evangelical Lutheran Church in America
  Department for Candidacy
  Division of Ministry
  Evangelical Lutheran Church in America
  8765 West Higgins Road
  Chicago, IL 60631-4195
  (312) 380-2877

Presbyterian Church (USA)
Office of Preparation for Ministry and Church
Vocations
Presbyterian Church (USA)
100 Witherspoon Street
Louisville, KY 40202-1396
(502) 569-5752

United Church of Christ
Office for Church Life and Leadership
United Church of Christ
700 Prospect Avenue
Cleveland, OH 44115-1110
(216) 736-2130

United Methodist Church
Division of Ordained Ministry
The United Methodist Church
P.O. Box 871
Nashville, TN 37202-0871
(615) 340-7400

Future Clergywomen... You Are Needed!

Remember that your religious tradition needs you. Large
numbers of clergymen are retiring, and well-qualified
women and men are needed to keep our churches and
synagogues thriving. Fewer men are entering the clergy,
and without the leadership of today's clergywomen, the
religious future of organized religion in this country
would be in trouble. If the schooling and steps necessary to ordination seem overwhelming, remember that
committed, caring clergy—perhaps like you—have important contributions to make to our religious communities and our society as we move into the next century.

4

Paths of Service

As an ordained clergywoman, many career paths lie before you. Even within a particular field, such as congregational ministry, a community's racial, economic, educational, and geographic conditions combine to make each placement unique. Add to these factors the individual gifts, abilities, and personality that each clergywoman brings to her work, and it is hard to find any two positions that are identical.

Some general guidelines and descriptions may help you understand the varied fields that clergywomen pursue. The thoughts and reflections of women from around the country are collected here to exemplify the insights and experiences of Jewish, Protestant, and Roman Catholic women engaged in religious work. The career opportunities outlined do not exhaust the options available to clergywomen. However, they do suggest the great variety of careers available in the ministry, as well as what each involves.

While reading about the career choices for clergy, you should consider which field is best suited to your talents and skills. For example, a person who speaks well before groups and would enjoy preaching might focus on a career as a congregational minister or rabbi. Someone who is a good listener might prefer to work as a pastoral counselor or a hospital chaplain. Someone who enjoys teaching might become a religious educator. A Jewish woman with exceptional singing talent and strong religious commitment might become a cantor. Those who are good at organization or administration might work with a religious agency. Someone who enjoys the atmosphere of a college might become a Hillel director or campus minister. As you consider your future career, think of your own preferences and abilities and how you might best serve your religious community (and yourself).

Another important consideration is salary. While ministers and rabbis earn enough to maintain a healthy life-style, they rarely become wealthy through their work. Christian clergy earn modest salaries that are sufficient to support themselves and their families. No one field of Christian ministry is notably more profitable than another. In Judaism, congregational rabbis earn more than their colleagues who work as chaplains. Clergy salaries also vary considerably depending on geographic area and your level of experience.

Salaries for Christian clergy cover a wide range. Starting cash salaries for a full-time congregational minister range from $10,000 to $25,000. This is clearly not competitive with other professional fields, but there are other substantial benefits. A typical ministerial package might include medical, disability, and life insurance, pension payments, education allowance, transportation allowance, and housing. Many churches own homes that they maintain for their minister. Typically these are fairly large, comfortable houses designed to accommodate families. When the church does not own a parish home (which may be called the parsonage, manse, or rectory, depending on the denomination), a pastor may receive a housing allowance.

A rabbi's starting salary is substantially higher than

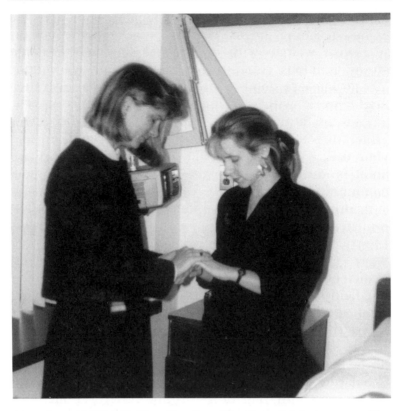

Rev. Anne Griffith (left), a Southern Baptist minister, prays with a family member of a hospital patient.

that of a minister. The graduates of a rabbinical school can expect to earn $35,000 to $45,000, with benefits of medical, disability, and life insurance, pension payments, and a convention allowance. A parsonage may be provided, but more commonly the rabbi finds her own housing. A set salary is offered to all Reform rabbis in their first congregational placement; for Conservative and Reconstructionist rabbis there is more variation depending on the position.

For both ministers and rabbis, salary increases accompany advancements. As your experience and expertise grow, you become eligible for better-paying positions. For a congregational minister or rabbi, this usually means serving larger congregations, which have bigger budgets and offer higher salaries. For a chaplain, it may mean moving to another campus, prison, or hospital or being promoted to a supervisory position. However, career advancement is generally more difficult for clergywomen than for clergymen. Some clergywomen become frustrated as they watch their male colleagues with the same experience move more rapidly to desired positions. Congregations that may be willing to accept a woman as an assistant or associate rabbi or pastor are often reluctant to have her as senior rabbi or pastor. Even clergywomen with decades of service encounter this discrimination. Some wryly refer to it as the "stained-glass ceiling." As in other fields, women in the clergy need to struggle for equality and recognition.

Whereas some clergywomen work toward advancements and salary increases as part of the natural progression of their career, others make conscious decisions to prioritize different needs. Some clergywomen place greater emphasis on the quality of their work (regardless of salary), or on coordinating the geographic restrictions of a spouse's career, over going wherever the best career move might lead them. Some clergywomen, especially those with children, opt to trade a "fast-track" career for part-time work that enables them to spend more time at home. Although men rarely worry about having a family and a successful career, most women who work outside the home are burdened by these concerns. The same is true for clergy. While clergywomen realize that these decisions result in career compromises, some find that they enable them to meet the demands of both their life-style and their professional goals.

While some of the realities of becoming a clergy-woman may be discouraging, becoming a minister or rabbi is still a very exciting and promising field for women. The fact that more women are entering the ministry than ever before shows that it is an attractive career despite predictable difficulties. The work of a clergywoman is stimulating and rewarding. Schedules are flexible and days are varied. Most of all, a clergy-woman generally loves and believes in what she does. Says one rabbi, "You have to love it. This work is too hard if you don't."

The following sections explore why clergywomen love their work, the frustrations they endure, and what various career fields involve. Fictional characters, created as composites of actual clergywomen, provide glimpses of a typical day in the careers. As you learn about the many possibilities available to clergywomen, you can begin to discover which career might be most fulfilling for you.

5

Serving a Congregation

When thinking of a clergyperson, you probably picture a minister or rabbi who works with a congregation, since that is what most clergy do. Serving a congregation places the clergyperson in a highly visible position in the community. It is also the role in which the news and entertainment media portray clergy most frequently. In the movies we usually see a clergyperson (more often than not a clergy*man*) performing a wedding or leading a service, wearing a long robe and looking rather serious. People who are not involved in communities of faith tend to assume that this is pretty much all that ministers and rabbis do. In real life, however, it is only one part of the work of a congregational minister or rabbi (who is no more or less serious than anyone else).

CONGREGATIONAL MINISTER
The responsibilities of a congregational minister (or pastor) vary greatly depending on the location and size of the congregation (or parish) and its economic, racial, and social conditions. A minister may be a solo pastor or serve as part of a ministerial staff. If she is in a multistaff position, her area of expertise may be designated by her title, such as Minister of Christian Education, Youth Minister, or Minister of Visitation.

Rev. Kate Parker-Burgard, a United Methodist pastor, officiates at a wedding (photo by Don Parker-Burgard).

Perhaps she is part of a ministerial team as the assistant, associate, co-pastor, or senior pastor. Her role as minister depends on her specific responsibilities, as well as the emphases she brings to her work through her own talents, interests, and skills. She also brings a love of her faith.

A Pastor's Responsibilities
The primary gathering place for a Christian congregation is at worship, usually on Sunday mornings. In this sacred time, the minister combines the elements of Scripture, music, prayer, silence, concerns, and preaching to celebrate the presence and power of God. Proclaiming the Word of God is an important part

of her role as a pastor, and she spends hours during the week preparing a sermon based on passages from the Bible but incorporating modern insights and timely illustrations. She meditates and prays earnestly as she prepares for each worship service. Communion may be celebrated each day, once a week, every month, or less frequently in her church. During this sacrament, the minister presides over the consecration and distribution of the elements (bread and wine) as the congregation joins in the ritual. Leading worship is a precious responsibility, and she is practically trained and spiritually prepared for the task and privilege.

Special services of worship also take place in the life of a church, usually revolving around distinctive moments in the congregants' lives. The minister officiates at baptisms, weddings, and funerals and is an integral part of these intimate times of celebration and mourning. These occasions give the clergyperson a chance to be with others and share their joys and sorrows. Many congregational ministers consider this one of the most cherished parts of their calling.

As the pastor helps to guide people through life changes, she also helps to teach members of her congregation about their common heritage of faith. She is an educator, and having studied the Bible, the history of Christianity, and the legacy of her own denomination, she shares her learning in many ways. Teaching is an integral part of her preaching, as she incorporates biblical insights and history into her sermons. She may also teach Bible studies or Sunday school classes, either to adults or to children. Maybe she prepares youth for confirmation as they study to become members of the church. She might coordinate a summer program of Vacation Church School, combining learning about the Bible and faith into a children's recreational period of fellowship. As she teaches, the pastor also helps her

Rev. Bonnie Perry, an Episcopal rector, celebrates the Eucharist.

students to incorporate their own valuable insights and experiences into their learning.

Another emphasis in a pastor's ministry may be pastoral counseling. Many people in a crisis turn first to their clergyperson because they know and trust her. She might feel qualified to help someone going through a temporary period of crisis but realize that certain problems rooted in long-term psychological abuse require extensive treatment. The amount of counseling that a pastor does depends on her training and ability, as well as on other counseling resources available.

To come to know the members of her congregation better, a pastor makes visits. She may take communion to older members who are unable to get to church. The minister visits hospital patients to offer support and consolation and to pray for healing and hope. If there are people who are interested in joining the church, the pastor might visit to extend an invitation. When a personal visit is not possible, the pastor talks with people by phone, letting them know that they are remembered.

Another important mode of communication that the pastor employs is writing. Most churches generate newsletters that are sent to members and friends of the congregation periodically (every month, week, or quarter). Recognizing the newsletter as a valuable tool of ministry, the pastor may oversee its publication, be in charge of its production, or write a column. She also writes to members of the congregation and others as needed. She may occasionally contribute an editorial to a local newspaper. Her writing skills serve her well as she helps maintain the connections that enable the church to thrive.

The minister tends to the church's spiritual growth and her own. She may set aside some time for personal daily devotion as she reflects on what is happening around her. Members of the congregation may ask her to serve as their spiritual director to guide them as they explore questions of faith. The pastor may organize retreats for the congregation to focus on deepening their relationship with God. She may coordinate small groups that meet to nurture one another and share prayers and concerns. The pastor is committed to spiritual development with her congregation.

Opportunities for spiritual growth, pastoral counseling, worship, community activities, increased learning, and various other church activities are made possible through the organization of the congregation and the facilities of the building. In most churches, the pastor finds herself functioning as chief administrator, overseeing operations, budgets, and committee work. In larger churches, the pastor may have the luxury of a separate staff person who functions solely as administrator, but that is rare. Many pastors find administrative work a frustrating way to spend their time. Some pastors enjoy it, however, as an opportunity to maximize the church's efficiency. Administration, while commonly overlooked in the work of a pastor, is essential to the ministry.

These are some of the many ways that a pastor fills her days, but there are countless more possibilities. These responsibilities develop from the needs of the community and the interests of the pastor and congregation, and they depend on the human and financial resources available. A pastor's work might include overseeing the building of a new church or repairs to the facilities. She might join or form a community task force on hunger, homelessness, or housing. She might be involved in interfaith work in the community. Perhaps she is active in denominational concerns and committees. A pastor who is talented in music or drama might create a choir or drama troupe. Limitless creative options are available to her.

What interests do you have? What variety of activities might you pursue as a pastor? If you enjoy exploring a range of ideas and involvement, that would be an asset in working with a congregation. At the same time, pastors need to be cautioned about overcommitment and a tendency to care for others but neglect themselves. Clergywomen who feel many demands are finding ways to manage the demands of their personal and professional lives as they seek to create a balanced life-style in which they and their congregations can grow and thrive.

A Day in the Life of a Congregational Minister

Rev. Kathy L. is a United Methodist pastor, working with an interracial congregation of about 200 members outside a large city. She is thirty years old, and she and her husband, Don, recently had their first child, Jacob. Don commutes to the city, where he works for an insurance company. This is a sample day in the life of a pastor.

The alarm goes off at 6:45 a.m. Kathy groggily reaches over to turn it off. "Missing sleep is the hardest part of being a mother," she thinks to herself, remembering how Jacob cried during the night. Fortunately the baby is still asleep, so she takes the opportunity to get up and get ready for the day. She wakes her husband, who needs to catch the 7:52 train into the city. The two of them, enthralled with their five-month-old son, look into the nursery at Jacob sleeping peacefully. "He looks like an angel, which he is," Kathy smiles to Don. "Of course, he'll soon outgrow that," she laughs. While the couple have a quick breakfast, they hear Jacob waking up. Don goes upstairs to say good morning to the baby and change his diaper. He then needs to leave for the train station, which is within walking distance. Kathy says good-bye to Don and carries Jacob to the door, trying to get him to wave to his Dad. Then she goes about feeding and dressing her son. At about 8:30 she loads the car with baby supplies for the day and drops Jake off at the home of the baby-sitter. A little before nine she returns home, parks the car, and goes into the house to make herself a cup of strong coffee. With steaming mug in hand, she walks over to the church office, which is next door to the parsonage. "Good morning, Mabel," she greets the church secretary, who works from nine to noon five days a week. "Hi, Pastor Kathy," Mabel responds, "how's the baby?" "Precious and restless," Kathy responds. Then turning her attention to church business, she asks, "How's the newsletter coming along?" "Just fine, except I'm having a hard time reading this note that Burt asked me to put in about the church fair." Kathy looks over the note and helps to decipher it with Mabel. Going into her study, she asks Mabel to hold all calls unless there is an emergency. She needs to work on her sermon for Sunday, and she wants to take advantage of Mabel's presence.

At her desk, Kathy begins her preparation with prayer. She then turns to the Bible and the passages that she plans to preach on at the end of the week. She consults biblical commentaries and resources about life in ancient times, and then writes down a few points for the sermon. She starts to jot down some ideas for modern illustrations when Mabel buzzes. "Pastor Kathy, sorry to interrupt you, but it's Tyrone Washington on the phone. He sounds very upset. His wife is getting worse." "Thank you, Mabel," Kathy says, and takes the call. She offers Tyrone words of comfort over the phone; his wife Evelyn is slowly dying of Alzheimer's disease. She then tells him that she will come by the hospital this afternoon to visit with them. When she turns back to her sermon preparation, she finds that she has lost her train of thought. She decides to tend to some administrative details and preparation for the evening's finance committee meeting. At least she has made a start on the sermon; maybe she can sit down to her computer the next day to begin writing.

That afternoon she goes to the hospital to visit with the Washingtons. Evelyn no longer recognizes the pastor, and Kathy realizes that she may die soon. Tyrone is not even sure that Evelyn recognizes him, and he is very distraught. Kathy feels that her most im portant role is to offer support to Tyrone and let him know that he is not alone in his ordeal. Before leaving, she and Tyrone each take one of Evelyn's hands and pray together.

Returning to her office, Kathy realizes that she has about an hour before she needs to pick up Jake. She checks the messages on the answering machine and calls back the chair of the finance committee, who has a few questions about the evening meeting. She remembers to call an elderly member of the congregation to wish her a happy eightieth birthday and takes the few remaining minutes to review the lesson that she will teach to the confirmation class the next afternoon. Soon she goes to pick up the baby and is delighted to see him again.

At home, Kathy finds a message from Don on the phone machine, saying that he has to work late. Kathy calls him at the office, and he explains that he has to meet a deadline on a project and won't be home until 8 or 8:30. They work out how to juggle care of Jacob while Kathy is at her 7:30 meeting. Without time to get a baby-sitter, Kathy decides to take Jacob to the first part of the meeting (even though he is inevitably a distraction), and Don can pick the baby up when he gets home. "I'll make supper and leave it for you to put in the microwave," Kathy tells her husband. "See you later."

That night Kathy goes to her meeting and helps the committee work out a budget. They strategize on how to raise funds for the church. Jacob is in his portable playpen and manages to amuse himself and gurgle quietly, for which Kathy is very grateful. The meeting goes well, and despite the difficult finances, people feel hopeful and committed to their future as a church.

Don comes in around 8:20 and takes the baby home. At 9:00 when the meeting is over, Kathy joins them back at the house. Don has already put Jacob to bed, so now he and Kathy have a little time to themselves to talk about their days. At 10:00 they watch the evening news together and then fall asleep until the next day (or until the baby wakes up).

CONGREGATIONAL RABBI

The rabbi who serves a congregation is also known as a pulpit rabbi. Much of the work she does is determined by her congregation's size, staff, and community. Since Judaism does not have a religious hierarchy, the particulars of her work vary substantially with the congregation that she serves. Most often one rabbi serves a synagogue; however, a rabbi may have a position on a larger staff as Assistant, Associate, Co-rabbi, or Senior rabbi. Whatever the situation, the rabbi is a teacher to the congregation, as she learns with her congregants and shares her knowledge and love of Judaism.

A Rabbi's Responsibilities

The rabbi is expected to lead *Shabbat* (sabbath) services on Friday nights and Saturday mornings. *Shabbat* is a sacred day for the family at home and the family of the synagogue. As the congregation comes together for worship, the service is provided in the *siddur*, or prayer book. The prayer book is printed in both Hebrew and English, and the rabbi's fluency in Hebrew helps to guide the congregation. As part of the weekly service, the rabbi preaches a sermon that is usually based on the assigned verses from the *Torah*, although it may incorporate passages and insights from the rest of the Hebrew Bible as well. Through worship and prayer, the rabbi calls Jews to appreciate the richness of their heritage while deepening their dedication to justice and devotion to God.

Preaching or giving a *d'var Torah* (word of the *Torah*) and leading worship are two of the many ways that the rabbi functions as a teacher. Emphasis on scholarship is integral to the history of Judaism, and the rabbi devotes time and energy to developing the educational opportunities of the synagogue. She nurtures a love of Judaism in the young people as she tutors them in reading the *Torah* and trains them to become a *Bar* or *Bat Mitzvah*. Working with adults, she might instruct in various Bible studies or other courses. The rabbi works with the temple's religious school and may serve as its principal. Writing is another method that the rabbi uses to teach, perhaps through a column in the congregational bulletin, or through articles, editorials, and outside publications. To be a rabbi is to be committed to one's own and others' learning.

Rabbis are called on to preside over life-cycle ceremonies such as baby-namings, weddings, and funerals. For the rabbi, these occasions offer the opportunity to get to know families in the congregation better. In these times of personal change, the rabbi helps to guide congregants through sad and joyous occasions with Jewish rituals, some of which have been used for thousands of years.

While building up Jewish tradition, the rabbi also tends to the pastoral needs of her congregation. She counsels those who are troubled and works with those experiencing crises. She makes referrals for those who come to her with problems that would be better addressed by a mental health professional. For a rabbi to refer a person is not to shirk her responsibilities; rather it is to make use of the help that is available and to act responsibly as a religious leader and guide.

The rabbi may visit members of the congregation, especially if someone is sick or has suffered the loss of a close relative. She maintains contact with those who are ill and visits hospitalized members of the congregation. Congregants do not expect the rabbi to pay calls routinely on everyone in the congregation, which in itself would be a full-time job. Rather, the rabbi and congregation together create a balanced pastoral style that serves the congregation and enables the rabbi to show her care and concern.

The congregational rabbi supervises the organization and daily life of the synagogue. This includes administrative tasks such as overseeing finances, working with committees, handling correspondence, managing maintenance of synagogue facilities, and generally supervising this center of Jewish communal life. Just how many of these duties are the rabbi's responsibility depends on the synagogue's resources. A large congregation, for example, may have a staff among whom administrative functions are divided. Some senior rabbis of large congregations find, however, that a big percentage of their time is consumed by administrative tasks. Often the president of the congregation works with the rabbi in performing some of these necessary jobs. If the synagogue is building a new sanctuary or constructing a wing on the educational building, the rabbi oversees this development. The rabbi works with the congregation to nurture a sense of community within itself, while reaching out to others.

The synagogue plays an important role in the community. The rabbi ensures the vibrant activity of the synagogue through its programming. She may invite outside speakers to discuss issues of concern to the Jewish community, such as Zionism, Israel and the Palestinian conflict, or themes in Jewish literature. The rabbi writes her column for the bulletin of the synagogue, which keeps the congregation informed of events in the life of the community. The rabbi may also organize retreats, symposia, panel discussions, parties, commemorative services, or other gatherings that bring the congregation together to grow spiritually, intellectually, and socially.

In the wider community, the rabbi may participate in interfaith organizations. Some communities in metropolitan areas have concentrated Jewish populations and a corresponding number of synagogues, but often the rabbi finds that she is the only Jewish clergyperson on a community interfaith council composed primarily of Protestants and Catholics. In such situations, she may choose to explain Jewish customs to those unfamiliar with them. She may participate in interfaith events with her clergy colleagues, such as an annual Thanksgiving Service. Like all clergy, the rabbi serves as an ambassador of her faith.

As she upholds her faith and shares her love of Judaism, the rabbi also strengthens the commitment of Jews to their heritage. As many Jews identify with their cultural tradition, the rabbi helps them to appreciate their religious tradition as well. For those who feel called to convert to Judaism, often through marriage, the rabbi is prepared to instruct and lead in the process. Through teaching and personal example, the rabbi invites Jews to active involvement in their community of faith.

If you are eager to learn and teach about Judaism, you might be one of tomorrow's rabbis. As a pulpit rabbi, you would share in some of the most agonizing and exhilarating moments of people's lives. At the same time, you would manage daily affairs of an organization that is devoted to serving the Jewish community. You would be involved in a wide range of activities that would leave you excited and, sometimes, exhausted.

As you consider becoming a congregational rabbi, remember that the demands are varied and extensive, and
you would need to care not only for the congregation,
but for yourself. As most rabbis today would agree,
however, there is no substitute for devoting your life's
work to your passion for Judaism.

A Day in the Life of a Congregational Rabbi

*Rabbi Naomi S. is the rabbi of Congregation Beth El, a
Conservative synagogue of 300 families in a metropolitan
area. She been serving this congregation for five years,
after working for three years as an assistant rabbi in
a large suburban congregation. She is single, and people
in the congregation are finally beginning to ease up on
match-making.*

By 7:00 a.m. on Monday, Rabbi Naomi S. is already
at the synagogue. It is time for the morning prayer
service, and the handful of congregants who come each
morning before work have gathered. She puts on a
kipah, a *tallit*, and *tefillin*[1] before entering the sanctuary.
When a *minyan* is present, Naomi leads them in prayer.
The small congregation gently sway to her rhythmic
chanting of the *Torah* as she reads from the Book of
Genesis. When the brief service is over, they chat before
leaving for work or home. For all of them, this is a
meaningful way to start the day.

Naomi walks home at about 8:15, thinking about the
passage that she has read from the *Torah*. Busy com-
muters rush by her cramming onto buses, but Naomi
is absorbed thinking about the story of Hagar and
how God comes to the aid of the outcast woman. The

---

[1] The *Kipah* is a skullcap; the *tallit* is a prayer shawl; the *tefillin*, or
phyllacteries, are small leather cubes containing verses from the
Torah, worn on forehead and upper arm.

Interfaith Council of her neighborhood is organizing a shelter for homeless women with children, and Naomi has noticed increasing numbers of homeless in the area over the past few years. At the last meeting of the Interfaith Task Force on Homelessness, someone from her congregation had suggested that they call the shelter "Hagar's Home." The council agreed that it was a very appropriate name and adopted it. The basement of St. Mark's Episcopal Church down the boulevard is to be used for the shelter, and on Tuesdays members of Congregation Beth El will staff it overnight and provide dinner for the twelve guests. Naomi thinks about this as she passes St. Mark's.

Once home, Naomi flips through the morning paper while having breakfast. She notices her own name under Community Events. Later that week at the library she is to present a lecture entitled, "Anne Frank's Frankness: Exploring her Passion and Pathos." This is the third time that she has addressed this luncheon group, composed mostly of senior citizens, and she looks forward to it.

After breakfast, Naomi returns to the synagogue. The thought crosses her mind, "How many times do I make this trip in an average day?" The synagogue is only half a mile from the brownstone apartment that she rents with her housing allowance. She walks whenever possible to get some exercise (and also to avoid hunting for a parking space when she gets home in the evening). Even though going back and forth wears her down at times, Naomi likes being close enough to home to get something she may have forgotten, to take time out in the day to think about a sermon, or just to take a break. She knows that she needs to be careful not to be consumed by her work, which is especially difficult for single rabbis.

By 9:30 Naomi is at her desk preparing for her

weekly *Talmud* class that meets the next night. The class is an ongoing series that more and more people have been attending over recent weeks. Now some thirty people gather as they continue to learn about *Yoma*, a section of the *Talmud* concerned with who should and should not fast on *Yom Kippur*, the Day of Atonement. Last week one of the members asked a particularly interesting question about pregnant women. Naomi made note of the point, and the group talked about it briefly, agreeing to discuss it further the next week. As she surrounds herself with familiar books from her shelves, she thinks how lucky she is to have work that pays her to study. She loves poring over the *Talmud* and looks forward to the evening class.

The morning is miraculously quiet, and Naomi is able to work with few interruptions. After about an hour of intense concentration, she hears the children from the nursery school trooping by her study on their way to the playground, and she gets up from her desk to greet them. "Hi, Matthew and Azar! Hi, Zack. Hello, Adina . . . now be sure to hold your partner's hand," Naomi smiles at the children. "Hi, Rabbi!" a chorus of little voices respond as they wave at her with their free hands. Naomi knows a number of these children and their families; she even officiated at a few of their baby-naming ceremonies. "I wonder if I'll still be at this synagogue when they become *b'nai* and *b'not mitzvah*," she thinks to herself. As the children file by, she hears Adina announce to her friend, "When I grow up, I'm going to be a rabbi too." Naomi smiles, grateful for the changes that have taken place over the past generation: The possibility of becoming a rabbi had never occurred to her when she was four.

That afternoon Naomi goes through the day's mail and responds to letters that demand immediate attention. She is grateful for the help of Linda, the synagogue secretary, who is cheerful, efficient, and helpful in typing and sending out correspondence. The rest of the afternoon is largely consumed by phone calls, as Naomi returns the pile of messages on her desk and follows up with a few congregants to see how they are doing. She also calls a lawyer, a doctor, and a priest from the community who are to join her on a panel program addressing the ethical questions, "When Does Life Begin? and When Does Life End?" Although there is much more work in her study waiting to be done, Naomi stops at a few minutes before four o'clock to get ready for a meeting with a couple who are planning to marry.

At four o'clock, Linda announces that the couple have arrived. They come into Naomi's study and exchange greetings. The woman, Susan, has been a member of Congregation Beth El her whole life, although she has not been active since she went away to college, then medical school; Naomi does not know her very well. Susan met her fiancé, Darrick, in medical school. They seem like energetic and considerate people, and Naomi is glad to meet with them. Early in the conversation, however, Susan explains that Darrick is Lutheran, and they would like to have a joint ceremony with Naomi and Darrick's pastor co-officiating. "There are some things that I need to explain to you," Naomi informs them gently. "In Judaism the wedding is part of forming a Jewish household. Both partners must be Jewish, so few rabbis will officiate at an interfaith service. In the Conservative movement, rabbis are not even allowed to do so." This takes Susan and Darrick by surprise. Naomi guides them through their confusion, answering their questions and asking them about their religious backgrounds. She listens closely to what they say about themselves, their religion, and visions for their life together. Naomi notices that Darrick has some fears about the marriage because of his own parents' divorce. She suggests that they might want to meet with a family therapist whom she knows at the Community Counseling Center. Both seem grateful for the suggestion. Naomi invites them to call her if they have any questions or would like to talk further. The couple thank the rabbi sincerely as they leave her study.

Naomi heads home, glad for a night to herself. She changes into casual clothes and calls Leslie, a college friend who lives nearby. "How about a movie tonight?" Naomi proposes. "Sounds great, I could use a little reality escape this evening," Leslie agrees. They plan to meet for supper at Ben's Kosher Deli, then take in a film. At the end of the evening Naomi is tired but happy and sets her alarm to go to *minyan* the next morning.

MULTISTAFF POSITIONS (MINISTERS AND RABBIS)
Assistant and Associate

One career option that many clergywomen choose, especially for their first position, is becoming an assistant or associate minister or rabbi. Generally this involves working with one other clergyperson, although in large churches or synagogues there may be several clergy on the staff. In Judaism, to be an associate is often an advancement from being an assistant. In Christianity, some denominations use only the term associate; others refer to an assistant or associate interchangeably. To work as either an assistant or associate with another minister or rabbi offers some distinct advantages but calls for some words of caution.

For newly ordained clergy, serving as an assistant or associate provides an opportunity to learn about the life of a congregation and to contribute to its leadership with the support of a seasoned colleague. Working with a senior rabbi or minister, the assistant or associate may gain the benefit of her colleague's wisdom and experience. She can become familiar with the administration and organization of the church or synagogue without being solely responsible for its leadership. She may be in charge of certain areas of programming or pastoral care, such as religious education, member visitation, or youth activities; but many tasks may be shared, such as conducting worship and chairing committee meetings. Serving as an assistant or associate can help a rabbi or minister develop her professional skills with the guidance of the senior clergyperson.

For women, an assistant or associate position is a popular option for many reasons. The ordination of women being relatively new, many women are in their first or early placements, which are more likely to be associate or assistantships. Some clergy choose to spend their entire career as an associate or assistant because they prefer working with larger congregations that offer a wider range of programs and services. A part-time assistant or associate position may also allow for attractive scheduling options for a clergywoman with young children. Some clergywomen enjoy working with a colleague with whom they can share ideas, planning, and reflections.

Yet some clergywomen report difficult experiences in these positions. A younger woman who is an assistant or associate may be perceived more as a daughter to the senior rabbi or minister, instead of a professional colleague. Also some senior clergy may be concerned about their own power and reluctant to share leadership. Some senior clergy try, even without realizing it, to impose their own tendency to overwork on their assistant or associate. If you consider such a position, first investigate whether the senior is someone with whom you could work well. You also need to be clear on what is expected of you—and what is not. If gaining

Rev. Kristen Soltvedt, a minister in the Evangelical Lutheran Church in America, with a clergy colleague, greets parishioners.

experience in preaching or officiating at weddings and funerals is important to you, ask if you will have those responsibilities. An assistant or associate is not a "gopher" or secretary or stand-by or student-in-training. One associate minister tells of her shock and dismay when a prominent member of her congregation asked when she was going to be ordained: She had been ordained three years earlier and had been serving as a pastor in that congregation for a full year. Congregants may well imitate the respect (or lack therof) that the senior pastor demonstrates toward the assistant or associate. However, when the associate/assistant and senior clergyperson get along well and share in caring for the faith community, this arrangement can be mutually gratifying for the clergy and the congregation.

Co-Pastors and Co-Rabbis

Some congregations that have two clergy on staff have co-pastors or co-rabbis. In these positions the two clergy have approximately the same amount of experience and earn comparable salaries. For clergy couples this arrangement may solve the problem of finding career placements in the same area. If the clergy couple have children, the husband and wife can share child-care and professional responsibilities. When one of the co-rabbis or co-pastors is a woman and the other is a man, whether they are married or simply colleagues, both need to be committed to modeling the equality of their positions. Because she is female, the clergywoman is not automatically the specialist in children's programs or the clergyperson of second rank. Instead she is a professional and an equal, working with her colleague to lead and to serve the congregation.

Senior Pastor or Senior Rabbi

The senior rabbi or senior pastor is an experienced and accomplished clergyperson who heads the staff of the synagogue or church. Many congregations that can afford two (or more) clergy realize the benefits of having both a man and a woman clergyperson to address different needs. Unfortunately, it is almost automatically assumed that the woman will be the assistant or associate and the man will be the senior minister or rabbi. Even women who have extensive experience in the rabbinate or pastorate are rarely hired as the senior clergyperson in multistaff situations. Yet some women who are already in these positions show by their actions that women are totally capable of fulfilling the role of senior clergy.

Since the congregations that have more than one clergyperson are generally large, the senior pastor or rabbi has many duties that she must oversee as she delegates responsibilities and completes many tasks herself. Preaching is often a central aspect of the senior clergyperson's work. She also needs strong administrative abilities to coordinate the many activities of her synagogue or church. The senior minister or rabbi communicates with her colleagues and congregants, welcoming their contributions and insights. With her guidance, a strong congregation continues to grow and thrive.

Cantors

Leading the congregation in singing the prayers that have been part of Jewish heritage for countless generations, the cantor is a clergyperson with special skills and musical talent. Traditionally, the cantor's role was solely that of a *hazzan*, one who chants the liturgy. This is still central to a cantor's contributions to the community, but the cantorate has evolved into a multifaceted position. Although she is a not a rabbi, a cantor is still a clergyperson. As part of her graduation from cantorial school, a cantor is *invested*, which is the cantorial equivalent of ordination. Both the Reform and Conservative movements in Judaism invest women as cantors. Like her rabbinic colleagues, the cantorial candidate studies and prepares extensively to reach her goal.

A future cantor's career begins with musical ability. She can sing well and has obtained her college degree, as well as having had musical instruction before beginning her cantorial studies. Often a cantor's undergraduate degree is in music or Judaic studies; many cantorial students also have master's degrees in music, although an M.A. is not necessary to enter a cantorial program. Still, a certain level of proficiency is expected in such areas as voice, music theory, sight-reading, choral work, and instrumental ability. Should a candidate show great potential but lack training, she may

be accepted to a program on condition that she complete certain musical requirements before beginning her
studies at cantorial school. The greater background a
cantorial student has—both musical and religious—the
better off she will be

Once at the school of sacred music, the cantorial
student begins a four- to five-year program in which she
studies music and Judaica. The first year of instruction
is spent in Israel, where the student increases her proficiency in Hebrew, as well as her knowledge of Jewish
music, culture, and religious heritage. Upon returning
to New York City (where both the Reform and Conservative cantorial schools are located), she continues
her studies of *nusach* (traditional music of Jewish prayer)
as well as Hebrew, religion (Bible, philosophy), and
liturgy (*Shabbat*, High Holy Days, and Festivals). She
takes voice and often instrumental lessons, while developing her abilities in sight-singing, harmony, and com-
position. When the student finishes the requirements
set by the school, she is invested as a cantor. Further
information about these programs can be obtained from
these cantorial schools:

Reform
   Director of the School of Sacred Music
   Hebrew Union College–Jewish Institute of Religion
   Brookdale Center
   One West 4th Street
   New York, NY 10012–1186
   Phone (212) 674–5300

Conservative
   Dean, Cantors Institute
   Seminary College of Jewish Music
   3080 Broadway
   New York, NY 10027
   Phone: (212) 678–8000

93

A Cantor's Responsibilities

The cantor plays an integral part in the worship, leadership, and life of the Jewish community. Each week she prepares to lead the liturgy of the services, whether it be for *Shabbat*, High Holy Days, Festivals, or life-cycle celebrations. She may use her own compositions in the synagogue. The cantor may also serve as choral director for choirs of different ages in the congregation. Through worship and instruction, she teaches both children and adults about the rich heritage of Jewish music.

Another important role of the cantor is that of educator. Perhaps she teaches classes at the religious school, or serves as the school's director. She may tutor *Bar* and *Bat Mitzvah* students as they prepare to chant portions of the *Torah* and *Haftarah*, readings from the Prophets. Further work with the young people might include teaching confirmation classes. One cantor says teaching is her favorite work. "I love teaching *Bar* and *Bat Mitzvah* students; I feel this is my strength. Every child is unique, and through teaching I have the opportunity to engage them and turn around how they feel about their faith." A cantor does indeed affect how members of the congregation feel about their faith as she shares her love of Judaism through the powerful medium of music.

The cantor also cares for the congregation pastorally. As clergy, she officiates at life-cycle events. She may offer premarital counseling to couples whom she marries, as well as being available to those in the congregation who come to her with problems. The cantor may also lead retreats. Perhaps she offers programs that she has developed herself or in conjunction with other members of the staff. Like the rabbi, the cantor has administrative tasks. She is part of the pastoral team that provides care and leadership to the congregation.

The presence of women in the cantorate is rather recent. The first woman cantor was invested in the

Reform movement in 1975 and in the Conservative movement in 1987. Women have already brought exciting new dimensions to the field. Congregations that initially resist the idea of a woman cantor usually come to appreciate her vocal, pastoral, and spiritual contributions. One woman cantor encourages young women to take on these roles. "The women's issues are minor in comparison to the need for women to be in the clergy. It has done so much already for the women in our congregations, and we help to create a sense of balance in worship, spirituality, and prayer."

Both the Reform and Conservative organizations of cantors, called the American Conference of Cantors and the Cantors Assembly respectively, admit women. The American Conference admitted its first woman in 1975, and the Cantors Assembly began admitting women in 1991. Previously almost all liturgies were written for male voices, and women either had to transpose the music or sing unnaturally high or low for their vocal range. With the admission of women, however, the cantors' associations commissioned pieces to accommodate women's voices. As well as providing needed music, this step recognizes the growing and lasting contributions of women in the cantorate. One woman who is a member of the Association of American Cantors observes, "Once the floodgates were open, women started pouring in. Now the joke has become, 'We're looking for a few good men!' "

Women who have entered these floodgates and become cantors love what they do. Many have had professional careers in music, especially in opera, before turning to the cantorate. Their love of Judaism and of music compels them to become cantors. One woman tells of her decision:

I always thought about becoming a cantor. I grew up in the Conservative movement, in which women

95

weren't fully accepted, so my cantor suggested that I go into opera. I used to hate singing in operatic performances on *Shabbat* or Passover. During graduate school I was the cantorial soloist at a Reform Temple, and I realized that this was for me. I love combining my musical talent and my commitment to Judaism in one career. I never imagined I could be so fulfilled by what I do.

Becoming a cantor might be a highly fulfilling career for you too. You would need talent, along with your commitment, but the rewards would be great. The starting salary is approximately $40,000 to $50,000, and the need for cantors increases your chances of getting a very good position. But far more important is the satisfaction of doing something that you believe in and enjoy. A cantor advises young women, "Consider the obstacles of being in the clergy last. If your heart and spirit tell you it is right for you—do it. All else will fall into place."

A Day in the Life of a Cantor
Cantor Rhonda K. is the cantor of Children of Israel, a suburban Reform temple of 500 families. Her husband, Greg, is cantor at another large synagogue nearby. The couple met when they were in cantorial school and now have three children, Jenny, 11, Isaac, 9, and Danielle, 6. Children of Israel has two rabbis on staff, Rabbi David L. and Assistant Rabbi Valerie G. Today is especially busy for Rhonda since it is Shabbat.

The early morning is spent getting the children ready for school. Greg makes their lunches while Rhonda sees that Jenny, Isaac, and Danielle are washed and dressed in time to catch the school bus. Danielle is excited because her class is talking a field trip to the zoo, and

Cantor Jenny Izenstark, a Reform cantor, recites the kiddush, *a prayer over the wine sanctifying the Sabbath.*

she chatters about seeing all the animals. While talking with her and checking on Isaac, Rhonda and Greg hurry the children along so they will get to the bus stop by 8:00. Once they are safely off, Greg goes to his temple.

97

Rhonda plans to do the same after her morning run of three to five miles. As she puts on her radio headset tuned to classical music and strides out the door, she reminds herself how essential running is for her physical and mental well-being. "I know this helps me sing better," she says to herself, happy to be outside and jogging.

A few hours later, Rhonda is in her study at the temple. It is Friday, and she has tried to keep her schedule fairly open since the evening will be busy and *Shabbat* comes early in these winter months. Rabbi Valerie G. stops by to give Rhonda a message. "*Shabbat Shalom* (a peaceful Sabbath), Rhonda!" Valerie just started working at the temple two months ago, and she and Rhonda are already becoming good friends. "Mrs. Weiss called again about Amy's *Bat Mitzvah* tomorrow. She sounded rather nervous." "Thanks for telling me, Valerie. I'll give her call." Rhonda smiles to herself, amused that Mrs. Weiss is so concerned about her daughter's chanting from the *Torah* when Amy herself is excited, but confident. Rhonda has been tutoring her for the past year and knows that Amy will do an excellent job. She picks up the phone to reassure Mrs. Weiss. After returning a few more calls, Rhonda goes home to go over her music for the service that night.

When she gets home, Greg is at the piano. She greets him and, with a smile, negotiates when she can have her turn at the baby grand. "I've already paid the sitter and sent her home," Greg tells her. "The kids are downstairs watching a video." Rhonda goes into the den to hug her children and listens gladly to Danielle's report of her trip to the zoo. While listening, she feels the tension between wanting to spend time with her children and having so many demands at the temple. If Rhonda had an hour to spare, Danielle would joyfully fill it with descriptions of the elephants and lions she saw. But Rhonda has only a few minutes, then needs to go upstairs to practice on the piano briefly and prepare the *Shabbat* meal.

Shortly after sunset the family gather at the dinner table. Rhonda says a prayer over the *Shabbat* candles as she lights them with Jenny and helps Danielle to light a candle too. Greg helps Isaac say the blessings over the *challah* (special bread) and the wine, and the children each drink a sip. The family enjoy their meal of gefilte fish, baked chicken, noodle *kugel* (pudding), carrot *tzimmes* (compote), and tea and chocolate *babka* (cake). After dinner Greg and Rhonda gather their music and get ready to leave for their synagogues. This week the children go with Greg to his temple. Recently Greg and Rhonda decided that they would take the children to their respective temples on alternate weeks so that the children could spend *Shabbat* with each of their parents. Rhonda says good-bye to them as she gets into her car and cannot help but miss being with her family this *Shabbat*.

Before the service, Rhonda warms up vocally. She then puts on her robe and prayer shawl and joins the rabbis at the *bima* (pulpit). Her voice rings out clear, strong, and full of feeling as she leads the congregation in the *Hash Kivenu* prayer (prayer for Divine Providence). The congregation loves Rhonda's singing, and now that she has been at Children of Israel for three years she feels fully accepted and very much appreciated. Rhonda notices the Weiss family seated in pews toward the front and smiles at Amy. After the service, Rhonda talks with the Weisses at the *oneg*[1] and shares in their anticipation of the next morning.

---

[1] *oneg (Hebrew)*—short for *oneg Shabbat*, literally, "enjoyment of the Sabbath," a reception after worship, usually with refreshments.

When Rhonda gets home it is late, and Greg is getting the children ready for bed. She reads them their favorite story, *"Ima on the Bima"* (Mommy on the Pulpit), and tucks them in. Then she and Greg go to bed themselves, to rest before the *Shabbat* service the next morning.

6

Serving an Institution

A clergywoman who serves an institution such as a hospital, prison, or college is known as a chaplain. In fundamental ways, her work is similar to that of a congregational minister or rabbi, for the heart of what the clergyperson does is care for others and share the love of God. Many of her responsibilities are like those of congregational clergy; the chaplain preaches, teaches, creates programs, prays, officiates, leads worship, counsels, administers, and provides pastoral care to the community. However, the setting is different. Unless the institution where she works has a religious affiliation, the chaplain meets people in a secular (nonreligious) environment where they might even be surprised to encounter her.

Patients at a hospital, students at a university, and inmates in a prison are all there for a specific purpose: healing, learning, or serving time. Because of that, the chaplain becomes involved in people's lives in a unique way. People's contact with her—whether it be during a hospital stay for surgery, during years in higher education, or while in prison—may be meaningful and affect the rest of their lives. One campus minister reflects, "I like meeting people 'where they are.' Students don't try to act pious around me but simply share their worries and hopes." A hospital chaplain comments, "I rarely work with folks who don't leave here feeling that their priorities are different. People who become very ill start thinking about what is 'not done' in their lives. Working here feels like holy ground, and I feel privileged to be with people at this time." And a prison chaplain says, "People here are in crisis. I value the chance to help see them through these difficult, and sometimes harrowing, times." As in congregational ministry, the needs and concerns of the community shape the work of the chaplain.

The community that a chaplain serves is that of the institution and all its members. It is largely a rotating population of patients, students, or inmates, which challenges the chaplain to get to know new faces and to establish relationships. One campus minister describes her work as "doing ministry to a parade." Those who work at the institution generally are there for a longer period of time, and the chaplain gets to know them also. Working in a secular community may be both refreshing and frustrating to the chaplain. On one hand, she appreciates the interaction with people outside of a formal religious setting; on the other she may find it tiresome to explain her role to those who have little, if any, religious background, experience, or interest. Her community is diverse and goal-oriented around providing the institution's services.

Like the others who work at the institution, the chaplain rarely lives in the community she serves. A college chaplain may live on campus, but more often chaplains have their own housing. Living away from the institution, chaplains may experience a greater division between their home and professional lives (and perhaps greater privacy) than a congregational minister or rabbi. Also a chaplain may have a schedule of set weekly hours. These differences between congregational and institutional settings make chaplaincy appealing to some clergywomen.

Women clergy often find that they are more easily accepted (and offered positions) as chaplains than as congregational rabbis or ministers. This is partly because institutional positions are less traditional and, as a result, more open to women. Because of limited finances, chaplaincy positions may be part time or low-paying or both. Some chaplains see this as unfair because their work seems less valued than that of a congregational rabbi or minister. For other chaplains, especially if they have young children, part-time chaplaincy positions may enable them to spend more time at home. Careers in chaplaincies offer opportunities for creativity and flexibility.

The chaplain's ability and training enable her to fulfill her responsibilities; ordination may or may not be necessary. For this reason, laypeople may also fulfill their religious calling as chaplains. A chaplain prepares for her duties either while she is in seminary or in later years when she decides to develop these professional skills. In some areas of institutional ministry, such as campus chaplaincy, training may be largely in internships, workshops, and on-the-job experience. Other positions, such as hospital chaplaincy, may require more formal education.

Some women who are interested in becoming clergy do not picture themselves leading a church or synagogue. Perhaps their religious tradition does not allow them to fulfill this role. Perhaps they want to serve the community of a hospital, prison, or campus. If becoming a clergywoman is attractive to you, but the congregational ministry or rabbinate is not, serving as an institutional chaplain may offer the excitement and challenges that you are seeking in your career.

HOSPITAL CHAPLAIN

A hospital chaplain is a trained religious professional who provides pastoral care to the hospital community. Her "congregation" comprises patients, medical personnel, support staff, and administrators; the chaplain is an integral part of the team of professionals who provide care to the sick. She may be a layperson or a clergyperson who has trained extensively for the work.

Usually, preparation for hospital chaplaincy begins with a theological education; a hospital chaplain usually has the Master of Divinity degree or has graduated from a rabbinical school. Generally, her training has continued through chaplaincy programs of the Association of Clinical Pastoral Education (ACPE), a national accreditation agency. Those who wish to study the skills of chaplaincy enter a program of study with guidance from experienced chaplains who have been certified as supervisors. The students then work toward completion of one or more units of Clinical Pastoral Education (CPE).

Clinical Pastoral Education is the foundational training program for various types of work in pastoral care, including hospital chaplaincy. A unit of CPE consists of at least 400 hours of supervised learning, completed full time during a summer or part time over the course of a year. A CPE program brings together students who want the hands-on experience of visiting patients combined with a theoretical and theological education. Students are divided into small groups that meet with a supervisor for discussion and reflection. Throughout the CPE program, students write word-for-word reports (called *verbatims*) of conversations they have had with patients or hospital personnel. They then share these verbatims with the group and receive constructive criticism. Seminars are held and resource people are brought in to discuss relevant issues, such as drug and alcohol addiction, therapeutic touch, or dealing with death and dying. While learning about professional ministry, the student also discovers more about herself. This understanding enables her to realize why she may react a certain way to a given situation and helps her respond to others' problems professionally, but with genuine care and concern.

Since training in pastoral care is a beneficial skill for many clergy, quite a few rabbis, ministers, and lay-people complete a unit of CPE whether or not they plan to become chaplains. The amount of preparation required to work as a hospital chaplain varies among hospitals. Generally, those who decide to specialize in hospital chaplaincy are expected to continue their CPE training for at least another "basic unit" and then complete approximately two advanced units. The advanced units are often residency programs in which the student works at the hospital full time for twelve months. The student pays tuition of a few hundred dollars while participating in a CPE program. As she reaches the more advanced levels, however, she may receive a stipend of a few thousand dollars for living expenses.

A Hospital Chaplain's Responsibilities

The primary focus of a chaplain's work is visiting patients and offering them company and counsel. Patients may call the chaplain on their own initiative requesting a visit, or someone on the hospital staff may ask the chaplain to spend time with a patient who seems distressed. Often the chaplain gets to know patients simply by stopping in their rooms and introducing her-self. She also becomes acquainted with their families and friends. The chaplain may help the patient inform the family about his or her medical condition. When a

Rev. Nancy Adams (right), a minister in the United Church of Christ, talks with a hospital nurse.

patient remains in the hospital for a long period of time, a deeper relationship with the chaplain may develop. When the patient returns home, the chaplain may follow up with phone calls. If the patient dies, the chaplain may help with burial arrangements and preside at the funeral. At a very intense period in the life of a person and a family, the hospital chaplain can be a strong source of counsel, comfort, help, and hope.

Although the chaplain concentrates on caring for patients, she also reaches out to others in the hospital in seeking to nurture a loving community. She might create a support group for nurses in a critical care unit who become sad and discouraged at facing death so frequently. The chaplain might develop community programs on health-care issues or questions of medical ethics. Leading worship services in the hospital, especially during the holidays, may be another of her responsibilities. The chaplain's position also involves some administrative tasks, such as writing memos and attending hospital staff meetings. She might teach a Bible study class for the staff, or facilitate a group of patients in a therapy session. The hospital chaplain is immersed in providing pastoral care.

Clergywomen who are hospital chaplains find the work stimulating and rewarding, but admit that it can be tough. One Roman Catholic nun who has been working as a chaplain for many years says she has never gotten used to ". . . the constant facing of sickness, sorrow, and pain, especially when babies or teenagers or young adults are involved." Another long-time chaplain agrees, "My work at a cancer hospital entails witnessing crises and much suffering. At times it can be somewhat overwhelming." Still, both these women have been hospital chaplains for over a decade and find that the benefits of what they do outweigh the emotional strain.

In spite of the pain they encounter, hospital chaplains find their work gratifying. A young chaplain testifies, "I appreciate being involved in the lives of those with whom I work to an extent that would not be possible in any other field (besides ministry)." Another reflects, "Even though it may sound strange, I like enabling people to resign themselves to their death. It's a hard time, and I'm grateful when I can be there to help." Being in close contact with people, the chaplain may be present when a patient's life is changed, whether through a new baby or a terminal illness. For many chaplains, this is an appealing aspect of hospital chaplaincy. "Most people I work with," one chaplain says, "go away feeling comforted, or better able to face the future knowing that God is with them." A hospital chaplain shares the love of God in a setting where counsel, comfort, and compassion are needed in the midst of fear, hope, and the unknown.

Hospital chaplaincy might be an exciting career for you. If you would like to explore the field, you should enroll in a Clinical Pastoral Education program when you are in seminary to learn first-hand what it involves. To get into a program you need to file an application and have an admissions interview. Investigate the hospital and the program you apply to, as each facility offers a different experience. For further information on the requirements of CPE programs, you can write the Association of Clinical Pastoral Education at the following address:

Association of Clinical Pastoral Education, Inc.
1549 Clairmont Road
Decatur, GA 30033
(404) 320-1472

A list of Jewish, Protestant, and Roman Catholic chaplaincy organizations can be found in the Appendix.

Hospital chaplains work in life and death situations daily. If you feel drawn to help others in health crisis situations, you might consider this field of the ministry. Some chaplains pursue the work because of their interest in medicine. Others are gifted as pastoral counselors and want to work in a setting where they can use their listening skills. The reasons for becoming hospital chaplains are varied, but all reflect a strong commitment to the field. One minister describes the impact of her work:

I like being a minister in a secular setting. I like opportunities to minister to people who don't expect to meet God in their life that day the way they do when they go to church. In an institutional setting people don't anticipate it; when it happens there's a lot of power in it. People go through liberation that they weren't looking for—it's a grace-filled experience.

And a rabbi simply adds, "I love my work as a hospital chaplain." It might be a career that you would love, too.

A Day in the Life of a Hospital Chaplain

Rev. Helen P. is a Presbyterian minister who has been a hospital chaplain for eleven years. She has been divorced for fourteen years and has raised her son, Andy, who is now a high school junior. She works at Wimberly General Hospital, a rural hospital with 320 beds serving three counties.

Helen wakes up, not to the sound of her own alarm, but to the music blaring from the clock radio in her teenage son's room. She puts on her robe and bangs on his door, calling, "Andy, time to get up." She peers in and sees that he is still asleep. How he manages to sleep through that noise is a mystery to her. Then a voice from under the covers says, "Ten more minutes, Ma . . ." Helen starts to get ready for the day, and soon Andy does the same.

Both mother and son leave the house at about 8:00 a.m. "Have some breakfast, Andy," Helen urges him. "Sorry, Ma, no time," he says, kisses her quickly on the cheek, then grabs his knapsack of books and runs out the door. Helen sighs and realizes that she has no time for breakfast herself. "I'll pick up a bite at the cafeteria," she decides and drives to the hospital.

As she brings her coffee, muffin, and morning paper up to the chaplains' office, Helen reads the headlines.

109

"RUSSIAN ROULETTE AT LINCOLN HIGH SCHOOL" the paper screams. Yet another student has tested positive for the HIV virus in this school in the next county. It brings the total up to five in the past month. Helen is angered by the implication that contracting HIV is a random occurrence, like the danger of Russian roulette. "Attitudes like that only promote hysteria. If people think they can get AIDS by chance, it encourages fear of people with AIDS. I'm going to write a letter to the editor," she decides. "And maybe I'll call the principal of the high school and see if I can be of any assistance."

Helen starts thinking about the two HIV diagnoses that took place at Wimberly. She was there to help break the news to the family of one young man. As the mother of a teenage son herself, Helen could feel his parents' anguish, and she remembers the deep sadness that had filled that hospital room. The teenager had gone home weeks ago and reportedly was doing well, but still his story is tragic.

Turning to the tasks of the day, Helen plays the tape of the answering machine for messages. Since she shares an office with the other two chaplains, Rabbi Micheal M. and Sister Mary C., Helen notes the messages for them. One patient, John, a man in his sixties who has been in the hospital repeatedly for a heart condition, has called to ask Helen to visit him. He is to have a pacemaker installed that day. "Um . . . Hi, Rev . . . I'm going under the knife today," John says with forced cheerfulness, "think maybe you could stop by . . . ?" Helen's heart goes out to John. Since his wife's death last year he has been very lonely; his only son lives across the country, and John does not see him much. She goes at once to the coronary care unit and visits with John for half an hour. Then she offers a prayer that his surgery may go well. She reminds him that God

110

is always with him, and when she leaves, John is much calmer.

She decides to visit other patients in that ward and spends some time with two new patients who seem a bit scared in the hospital surroundings. Before heading back to the chaplains' office, Helen stops to chat with the nurses at their station. They are eager to tell the news that one of the nurses from their unit has just had a baby. "It's a boy!" they exclaim. "Barbara had a healthy little son!" "We're going to The Jolly Tavern to celebrate Friday night after work. Want to come?" one of the nurses offers. "Of course, Barb won't be there, but we know she'd want us to have a beer for her, too," she laughs. "Sounds great, I'd love it," responds Helen, knowing that Andy will be out with his friends on Friday night and she will not be missed at home. As she walks down the corridor to the elevator, Helen thinks admiringly of the nurses. "They work hard; they play hard," she smiles to herself.

The rest of the day flies by. Helen has a staff meeting with her colleagues about a program they will be starting next week. Some of the doctors and nurses had recently come to the chaplains asking for help in how to tell patients and families about difficult diagnoses, particularly of terminal illnesses. Micheal, Mary, and Helen decided to organize a series of lunch-hour discussion groups, "The Diagnosis Dilemma: How to tell them with honesty and care." They spend some time planning the format and delegate the various leadership components of the program. Before going home, Helen stops by the maternity ward. She sees that Barb is asleep and decides not to disturb her, but she looks in the nursery window at Barb's baby, Adam. Just to see him lifts her spirits.

At home, Helen finds Andy doing his homework, again with loud music playing. She stops in his room to

111

say hi, and they agree to send out for Chinese food, since neither likes to cook. Over supper they talk about the Lincoln High School cases of HIV. Andy had competed in track with one of the guys who tested positive. With the cartons cleared away, Andy goes to watch television and talk on the phone. Helen makes herself a cup of tea and reads a mystery novel. Before going to bed, she says a prayer for John and for the students with HIV and their families, and she thanks God for the birth of Adam and for the gift of her own son.

PRISON CHAPLAIN

In an environment of steel bars and separation, a prison chaplain seeks to create a caring community. She may or may not be ordained, but she is theologically trained and her beliefs lead her to help those shut off from society. The setting of her work may range from a small county jail to house prisoners being held on bail or for lesser crimes, to a large federal penitentiary with convicted inmates serving long sentences. (For convenience, jails, prisons, and penitentiaries on local, state, and national levels are all referred to as "prisons" in this chapter.) The particular circumstances of where she works affect her position greatly, but regardless of the setting, her congregation consists of inmates and the prison personnel. A chaplain who is a woman may serve either the male or female population of the prison, or both, depending on the facility.

There are different ways of becoming a prison chaplain. Usually, training is through a Clinical Pastoral Education (CPE) program, which provides hands-on experience in a course of supervised study. Since there are far fewer CPE programs in prisons than in hospitals, many prison chaplains develop their pastoral and counseling skills in a hospital, then apply them in a prison. Students work in an institutional setting and reflect on their experiences in a small group of peers with guidance from a chaplain supervisor. To obtain more information about CPE programs, you can write the Association of Clinical Pastoral Education at this address:

Association for Clinical Pastoral Education
1549 Clairmont Road
Decatur, GA 30033
(404) 320-1472

Depending on the correctional facility, the chaplain may have to fulfill extensive requirements before she can start work. Federal and state chaplains are law-enforcement officers and receive training as such when they are hired. To work in a federal prison, all personnel, whether a secretary, cafeteria worker, or chaplain, are trained in self-defense and law-enforcement procedures. The prison chaplain becomes a federal employee, eligible for advancements, transfers, and benefits within the national prison system. One chaplain says that she appreciates the "family atmosphere" that the prison system tries to promote among the staff. Since the population is more permanent at a federal prison than at a city or county jail, there are more opportunities for programs in such areas as education or alcohol and drug rehabilitation.

County and city prison chaplains usually receive their training on the job after their work in CPE. Often an interest has spurred them to investigate this career, and their ordination or other religious training qualifies them for the position. One chaplain says her desire to work in prisons began before her ministerial studies. She reflects, "Prison ministry became a love of mine when I did a master's degree in sociology. It became a reality when I prayed that God would open a door to

113

prison chaplaincy if God wanted me there. God opened the door, and I walked through."

A Prison Chaplain's Responsibilities

The prison chaplain provides worship experiences, pastoral care, and counseling to people who sorely need it. Inmates who are cut off from family and friends often experience great pain, guilt, and lack of self-confidence, in addition to the legal battles and personal problems that plague their lives. For women who are prisoners, there is an added dimension of sorrow since many are mothers. In New York State, for example, three out of every four incarcerated women have children. Observes one prison chaplain, "When a woman does time, the entire family does time with her." Women in prison are often worried about their children, who may be living with a relative or in a foster home. A chaplain can be a sympathetic link to "the outside."

The prison chaplain counsels inmates. Perhaps a prisoner is worried about her or his trial, and the chaplain listens to those concerns. The chaplain may also help prisoners get medical attention if they have a health problem that has been neglected. Sometimes the chaplain simply invites the prisoners to vent their frustrations or anger. Perhaps she offers a prayer and helps prisoners to be aware of God's presence in their struggle. She treats those who are imprisoned with the dignity and respect that they may feel are lacking in their lives.

To help inmates realize how valuable they are in God's sight, the chaplain conducts worship services. She may lead worship on a regular basis or during holidays and invite local clergy to come to the prison and preach. Music and singing are found to be uplifting to the prisoners, so the chaplain might direct a religious choir. For those imprisoned, worship offers a precious oppor-

Rev. Lillian Frier Webb, a minister in the African Methodist Episcopal Church, visits prisoners (photo courtesy Long Island Council of Churches).

tunity to gather as a community and hear a message of hope.

In addition to worship services, the chaplain creates programs for prisoners. She may teach a Bible study class or form a support group. Perhaps she designs practical workshops or spiritual retreats to interest and uplift prisoners. The chaplain may coordinate volunteer programs in which those who are not imprisoned help those who are. For example, churches or synagogues might collect needed items, such as toiletries, for prisoners. Members of a congregation might form a partnership with a woman prisoner and write her, visit her, and be an advocate for her in court. Prison chaplains provide the contacts that make such relationships possible.

If you are interested in becoming a prison chaplain,

115

certain traits and abilities would serve you well. Since you would be serving people of varied religions, you would need to be sensitive to their faith traditions. Women who are prison chaplains agree that one doing this work must not be judgmental, but instead needs to acknowledge her own ability to do wrong. Since many crimes are related to poverty, the chaplain realizes that under different circumstances she might be driven to the same desperation that led to the crime. At the same time, the chaplain's sympathy and understanding for the prisoner's situation need to be combined with "street smarts." People who are in prison have usually led tough lives that have taught them to survive by whatever tactics are necessary, including flattery and manipulation. Yet, in spite of this possibility, the prison chaplain is ready to listen to inmates when there seems to be no one else who will.

To assess your interest in becoming a prison chaplain, you might investigate the career by researching the prisons near your home. Find a county or city jail that has a chaplaincy program and try to arrange a meeting with a prison chaplain. Perhaps you could volunteer to help with worship services or programs. Since the environment and tight security of a prison often are intimidating, this would give you the opportunity to discover whether it is an atmosphere in which you could feel capable of fulfilling your vocational goals and religious calling. Perhaps you will find, as did one prison chaplain, "This is what I was meant to do!"

A Day in the Life of a Prison Chaplain

Sister Maria M. is a chaplain at Weir State Prison. She is Roman Catholic and lives with five other sisters in a convent not far from the prison. Maria has been working here, primarily with women inmates, for nine years. She became a prison chaplain after serving for fifteen years at an inner-

city parish. There she worked with many women who came out of prison and found their lives in shambles. Maria was attracted to prison chaplaincy hoping that if she could share the love of God with people in prison, she might help them to cope later with life "on the outside."

Sister Maria gets to the prison around noon and waves to the security guards. They know her well and greet her. "How different it was when I volunteered here many years ago," she thinks. "The security checks took so much time before I could get to the prisoners." She walks to the small office that she shares with Jacqueline, a social worker. While Maria and Jacqueline get along well, Maria is relieved that Jacqueline is on her lunch break so that she can have some quiet time to finish preparing for this evening's midweek worship service. On Sundays a priest comes to celebrate Mass, but on Wednesdays Maria leads an ecumenical worship service that is always packed. Maria looks over the Gospel lesson in Luke 4:16–21 and makes notes for her sermon. Every week she looks forward to this service.

With the sermon sufficiently prepared, Maria walks the tiers, or walkways, lining the prison cells. Some inmates call out greetings, eager for comfort or conversation. One woman, Carmen, beckons Maria toward her cell.

"Hermana, mira, venga aquí. Tengo una pregunta. Estoy tan aburrida... ¿me podrías conseguir una Biblia, por favor? Quiero leer los salmos," Carmen says.

"Okay, Carmen," Maria responds. *"Si quieres leer la palabra de Dios, te consigo una Biblia. ¿Sabes leer inglés?"*
Maria thinks of the stack of Bibles that she has in

117

her office. They were donated by a nearby church, but they are all in English.

"Un poquito. Pero puedo tratar. Lo importante es tener la palabra, ¿verdad que sí?"
"Es una cosa tenerla, pero es diferente poder entenderla," Maria smiles. *"Claro que te consigo una Biblia. No hay problema. Que Dios te bendiga,"* she says as she moves on.

(Translation:

C: Sister, come here. I have a question for you. I'm so bored . . . could you get a Bible for me please? I want to read the Psalms.

M: Okay, Carmen. If you want to read the word of God, I'll get you a Bible. Do you know how to read English?

C: A little bit. But I can try. The important thing is to have the Word, isn't it?

M: It's one thing to have it, but it's another to be able to understand it. Sure I'll get you a Bible. It's no problem. God bless you.)

As she walks on, Maria cannot help but wonder if Carmen really wants to read the Bible or just wants it to trade with another prisoner for cigarettes. Since Carmen didn't seem to mind if the Bible was in English, which she claims she can read a little, Maria is skeptical. But then again, she did mention reading the Psalms. Regardless, Maria does not want to refuse a request for a Bible, so she determines to find a Spanish Bible for Carmen.

Maria is called over by another inmate, Roberta, who is crying. "Chaplain," Roberta says quietly, "I need a prayer." Roberta is a crack addict, and this is her second prison term. After she got out last time, she returned to her drug habit, stealing to pay for it. Today she received a letter from her mother, who is taking care of Roberta's two small daughters. It has left her very upset. Howard, the father of the girls, who is also a crack addict, came to the apartment when he was high. He beat the girls and screamed about how horrible Roberta was and how she was hiding money from him. Roberta tells Maria that she almost wishes that she did not know about such awful scenes, because there is nothing she can do. What should she write to her mother? How can she help her daughters? What is going to become of them? Will they ever love their mother? Roberta asks these questions between sobs. Maria wishes that she could give easy answers, but there are none, and so she spends time with Roberta listening to her. Maria knows the Catholic Church in the inner-city neighborhood where Roberta's mother lives. She describes the parish outreach program there and suggests that Roberta write her mother that she can go to this church for help. Maria does not know if it will do any good, but it is worth a try. Yet Maria does believe in the power of prayer, and she is glad that Roberta asked to pray. They hold hands between the bars and Maria offers a prayer.

After more walking and talking and praying with prisoners, Maria goes back to her office. There she munches on the chicken sandwich that she brought as a supper break, before going to the recreation room for the worship service. Space is scarce in the prison, and there is no separate room for worship or religious activities. When services were first getting established in the rec room, Maria had to contend with prisoners who wanted to watch television while the service was in progress. Now, however, the prisoners and staff have more respect for this worship time. The setting does not look "holy," with bulletin boards and a Coke machine behind the podium that serves as a pulpit, but Maria has some of the women working on large religious banners that they will be able to drape over the machine. Regardless of the room's current appearance, Maria believes that the Holy Spirit is present.

As the service begins, the inmates filter in and pull up plastic chairs. Maria notices that Roberta is here for the first time. As she reads from the Bible and preaches on Jesus' message of liberation and justice, Maria looks at this congregation of women in regulation overalls and feels that they are listening hard. But the power of the service is felt most strongly through song. When the choir belts out a soulful rendition of "Amazing Grace," Maria sees tears in the eyes of quite a few women. And she feels them well up in her own eyes.

After worship is over, Maria feels uplifted by the service, but also exhausted. Emotionally and physically, it has been a demanding day. She leaves the prison at nine o'clock and goes home to the convent. One of the other nuns, Sister Eleanor, is just getting back from the elementary school where she teaches, after evening meetings with parents. She and Maria go to the kitchen and, over bowls of chocolate ice cream, share the stories of their days. Together they say the Liturgy of the Hours (a devotional reading of the Psalms) and then go to their rooms, grateful for the support of sisterhood.

CAMPUS CHAPLAIN

Working in a diverse community of people who have come together to learn, the campus chaplain helps students to grow spiritually as they grow intellectually. The Jewish student organization on campus is called *Hillel*, and the rabbi or layperson who runs the program is the Hillel director or advisor. Christian campus chaplaincy programs may have a name corresponding to a denomination, such as the Wesley Foundation (United Methodist), or be called the campus parish or campus ministry center. Regardless of her faith, the campus chaplain provides pastoral care and guidance to the students, faculty, and staff as well as offering programs and being involved in the life of the college or university.

As with other institutional chaplaincies, many of the responsibilities of the campus chaplain are shaped by where she works. She may be chaplain at a private rural college with a thousand students or at a large urban university with tens of thousands of students. The chaplaincy office may consist of one chaplain who works with people of various religions, or it may have several chaplains of different faiths. In some situations, especially if the school has a religious affiliation, the chaplaincy may be prominent on campus. On other campuses, the chaplain may feel that she needs to work hard to make the university population aware of her presence. Through opportunities and challenges, the campus chaplain appreciates the chance to work with students at this formative time in their lives.

Many campus chaplains enjoy the college or university community because the atmosphere is filled with new ideas. Some clergy say that it was their own involvement in campus chaplaincy that led them to become ministers or rabbis; as a result, they became chaplains themselves. Some like the mix of cultures that exists on a campus or simply the feeling of being at school. Says one campus chaplain, "School was always a place where I could do well. I like books, I like the smell of books. The university environment is good for me."

If you discover when you go to college that you enjoy the environment and you think you might be interested in this field, you probably will be glad to know that to start in a campus chaplaincy position does not require specific chaplaincy training. A minister's or rabbi's theological education and professional abilities equip her to begin this work. Many campus chaplains receive their training while in the position or from a predecessor and through workshops, conferences, and seminars. You can find out more about the resources that your denomination or movement offers by writing its office of higher education. There is also a list of chaplaincy organizations in the Appendix.

A Campus Chaplain's Responsibilities

Think ahead to when you go to college. When you arrive on campus, you may feel a little overwhelmed, especially if you are away from home and do not yet know anyone. There is so much to do and learn and so many new faces to get to know. At an orientation gathering, you meet the campus chaplain. Imagine that she or he is of your religion, so you already have something important in common. Through the chaplain, you get to know other students of your religion. Over time you become part of a community in which you feel right at home on your campus. A campus chaplain's job is to help create this community.

A campus chaplain reaches out in many ways to students as well as the faculty and staff. She may counsel those facing problems and pressures. She may lead worship services regularly or on holidays. A campus chaplain may perform weddings and occasionally other ceremonies. A large part of her work is creating programs that bring people together. These could range from small gatherings of student support groups to large university-wide rallies. The chaplain may lead programs in the dormitories or in an off-campus retreat. Some of the activities she schedules may be purely social, such as field trips or parties; others may be spiritual, such as memorial servies or prayer vigils. A campus chaplain often speaks before groups, and she may teach an academic course or be a guest lecturer. A Hillel director or campus minister contributes to the life of the university as she builds a religious community.

Current campus chaplains suggest that certain personality traits are helpful for this line of work. A self-starter who can take the initiative would be well suited for campus chaplaincy. A chaplain should not get discouraged easily; university students have demanding schedules, and at times she might feel that her programs are overlooked. If you are a creative person, however, campus chaplaincy can offer the chance to develop your ideas in a climate of learning and excitement.

A Day in the Lives of Two Campus Chaplains
Rabbi Nicole E. and Rev. Sara S. work together on the chaplaincy staff of Thayer University, an urban school with 10,000 students. Nicole is a Reconstructionist rabbi who has served as Hillel director here for four years. Sara, an American Baptist minister, started working at Thayer this fall. The chaplaincy center is composed of the Hillel office, the Protestant Campus Ministry, and the Campus Catholic Parish, which is headed by Father Jim. This is the last week of the fall semester.

Nicole's day begins early with a conversation and a cup of coffee in the student cafeteria. Lory, a first-year student, is worried because she is just ending her first semester and she is afraid that she will fail biology. "What are my parents going to say?" she sighs, holding back tears. "I don't know if I can make it at this school. Maybe I should transfer . . ." Nicole listens to Lory and reassures her. "Lory, starting out someplace new requires adjustment. With all the demands on you

123

Sister Dorothy Marnell (right), a Catholic campus chaplain, talks with college students.

academically, as well as changes socially, it's easy to feel overloaded. You still have your final exams . . . you may do real well. Study hard and be careful how you organize your time." Lory talks a bit more about her parents and then leaves for her morning class a little before 9 a.m. As Nicole walks toward the Hillel office, she thinks to herself, "For all the times I meet students here, I sometimes think this cafeteria is the 'Hillel Annex'."

Back at the chaplaincy center, Nicole sees Rev. Sara, who looks very distressed. "Sara, what's the matter?" Nicole asks. "There's been an ugly racial fight on campus," Sara explains. "Last night two black students were beaten up at a party. People had been drinking, and a group of white guys started picking on this black student because he is going out with a white

124

woman. His friend tried to help him and ended up in the hospital with three broken ribs ... Why does it seem that we haven't really come that far?" she sighs, more to herself than to Nicole. "This racist violence makes me so angry." The phone rings; it is Herb, president of the African-American Student Organization (AASO). Sara is the advisor for the AASO, and she and Herb agree to meet and discuss what they can do in response to this incident. Nicole offers to help in any way possible, perhaps creating a campus-wide event, then stops in Father Jim's office to let him know what has happened. Jim also asks how he can be involved, and the chaplains agree to meet the next morning to discuss the matter further, after Sara has spoken with Herb and the school administration.

Sara spends the morning talking about the racist outbreak with students in the AASO, as well as the dean of students and the president of the university. She had planned to spend the time preparing for the Christmas party that afternoon, and suddenly she feels very rushed. About thirty Protestant students are to gather at four p.m. for Christmas carols and cookies. With the help of Ernie, a Protestant student, Sara collects the tablecloths, decorations, cookies, and songbooks and sets up for the gathering. But last night's incident weighs heavily on her mind. "Tidings of comfort and joy," she thinks to herself ironically. "How can we make those real?" When the students start arriving, a number of them are also concerned and saddened by what they have heard about the fight and ask Sara what she knows. Rumors have been flying, and they are not sure what to believe. When they start to sing Christmas carols, however, the words "peace on earth, goodwill toward all" seem more meaningful.

Nicole is also organizing a holiday celebration, since tonight is Hillel's annual Chanukah dinner. The food has been ordered from a kosher caterer. When Nicole goes to the multipurpose room, she finds the caterer already there setting up, with help from Meir and Sharon, two students active in Hillel. Nicole places the menorah (candlabrum for nine candles) at the head table and pulls two bags out of her large pocketbook: one of plastic *dreidels* (spinning tops) and one of chocolate *geld* (money). As the students start arriving, they notice the bags and look forward to the *dreidel* contest after the dinner and celebrating the Chanukah story. A few university staff members also stop by, and the group passes an enjoyable evening lighting the menorah, telling the story of the Maccabees and the miraculous festival of light, singing Chanukah songs, and then spinning dreidels. By the time the party is over and everything is cleaned up, Nicole is tired and gets ready to leave the university.

She and Sara run into each other on the way to the parking lot. "Sometimes I wonder if *this* is what really brings the people of the university together," Nicole says with a smile, "a need for parking." Sara laughs, but she is thinking of the racial fight and that a sense of unity really is lacking. She is tired and knows that tomorrow will be a hard day with more strategy sessions over how to respond to the violence. Sara and Nicole wave good-bye as they get into their cars. "See you tomorrow," Nicole calls. "And Sara," she adds, noticing her colleague's expression, "take care of yourself. Really." "Thanks, Nicole," Sara musters a smile. "You too," and they drive off.

7

Serving in Other Ways

While many clergywomen develop careers serving a congregation or an institution, there are still other possibilities. They are hard to categorize under a specific heading because they cover a wide variety of opportunities. Clergywomen may work in these careers serving a congregation or an institution, or they may work independently. For example, a religious educator might develop programs for a congregation, teach at a seminary, or write resources for a denominational agency. A pastoral counselor could be on the staff of a congregation, or a counseling center, or in private practice. A mission worker might coordinate a community center in an inner city or teach prenatal care in a small village of a developing nation. An agency executive might preach in a local congregation one week and fly halfway around the world for an international meeting the next. A brief look at these options can help you to explore some of the remaining possibilities available to women as clergy.

As you consider these options, think about your own skills and areas of interest. What do you enjoy doing? How do you think you could best serve others, yourself, and your community of faith? Although clergywomen's careers are diverse, they have this in common: They are all fulfilling and rewarding. Clergywomen serving in any of many ways dedicate themselves to work in which they believe wholeheartedly.

PASTORAL COUNSELOR

The pastoral counselor is a mental health professional who comes from a religious tradition and has been specially trained. She may be an ordained minister or rabbi or a layperson. Like other mental health professionals—psychologists, social workers, or psychotherapists—the pastoral counselor's goal is to help her clients work through whatever is causing them distress. However, the pastoral counselor is distinguished from these colleagues because, along with training in behavioral sciences, she incorporates wisdom and insights from a faith perspective. That is not to say that she always responds by talking about religion, but rather she brings a pastoral approach to her work. One pastoral counselor describes her method: "I don't bring up religious questions, but I am attentive to hear if the client does. If so, we take it from there."

A pastoral counselor listens to clients with a trained ear. Countless issues may be brought to her—an abusive situation involving alcohol, drugs, or violence; problems in relationships with a spouse, friend, parent, or child; or a trauma such as the loss of a loved one. To help the client work through these difficulties, the pastoral counselor meets with him or her for a set period of time (usually about an hour) on a continuing basis. A client may need only a few sessions or therapy over a year or more. The sessions may be one-on-one, or with a couple or a family. Counselors' fees vary widely; many counselors offer a sliding scale according to the client's income. In some instances, the counselor recommends that the client seek treatment from another source, such as a psychiatrist, who is also a medical doctor.

Rev. Catherine Ellenwood, a Presbyterian minister, counsels a client.

Conversations between counselor and counselee are strictly confidential, as are the counselor's written records. Some pastoral counselors also give lectures or workshops on topics such as grief, anger, forgiveness, loss, abuse, violence, and loneliness. Whether address-

129

ing groups or counseling with individuals, the pastoral counselor's goal is to help people work through their problems toward happy and fulfilling lives. One counselor describes her work in this way:

> People in our society reach to fill emptiness in themselves. Sometimes they reach for the wrong things to fill that empty spot, such as drugs, overwork, money addiction, or affairs. The pastoral counselor helps the client search for spirit and relationships to fill the emptiness instead. It is like wading out with a person into deeply troubled water with the assurance that the client will not drown. The pastoral counselor must stay grounded in the deep water.

To do this, the pastoral counselor is professionally trained. Many pastoral counselors advise that a candidate should first be counseled, so she can learn about herself since she will be helping others to learn about themselves. The amount of experience and study necessary to become a pastoral counselor varies, but generally the counselor has at least a college degree and a graduate degree such as the Master of Divinity or a certificate of rabbinic ordination. Often she has a graduate degree in counseling as well. The organization that certifies pastoral counselors is the American Association of Pastoral Counselors (AAPC). The association requires that its members hold at least three degrees, demonstrate their competence, and be in good standing with their religious denomination or movement. If you would like more information about the AAPC, write to them at this address:

American Association of Pastoral Counselors
9504A Lee Highway

Fairfax, VA 22031-2303
(703) 385-6967

Are you a really good listener? Do your friends turn to you with personal problems because you are able to help them? Can you guide people to see the choices before them without telling them what to do? If so, you have some of the characteristics that make an effective pastoral counselor. As one counselor observes, "In this work you learn to be really present with people. You work with them as they work through their problems and discover the answers in themselves." As a pastoral counselor, you might help people to discover their own answers as they seek to achieve health, wholeness, and happiness in their lives.

RELIGIOUS EDUCATOR

Creatively passing on her tradition, the religious educator helps individuals and communities to explore their faith and heritage. She uses her teaching skills to transmit her knowledge through one of many vocational options. For example, a religious educator may work with a congregation, overseeing its educational programs. Perhaps she is a principal or teacher at a religious school. Some religious educators are scholars and teach in colleges or seminaries. Others instruct mainly through written materials or resources that they develop for schools or congregations. A religious educator may work with a specific age group, such as youth, small children, or adults. Yet regardless of the age she teaches or the position she holds, the religious educator invites and challenges her students to learn and grow as she continues to learn and grow herself.

Although all clergy teach about their religion, she who specializes in religious education has additional training. In seminary she might take courses in teach-

131

Dr. Lillian Bozak-Deleo, a Catholic professor, teaches a college theology class.

ing methods, curriculum development, and administration. She might choose these classes as electives while she works toward completion of her rabbinic studies or her Master of Divinity degree, or she might obtain a separate graduate degree in education. Some schools offer combined degrees for students who work toward ordination while planning for careers as educators. Whether or not a joint degree is appropriate depends on the role that the student envisions for herself. For example, one who intends to become a college or seminary professor would go on to obtain a Ph.D. (Doctor of Philosophy) in her area of concentration. Someone who wants to teach at a Jewish day school might get a Master's in Jewish Education. Also as part of her seminary experience, the religious educator would seek a field placement that enables her to develop her teaching abilities in a practical setting. She prepares herself academically and professionally so that she can effectively represent her tradition.

In past decades, women were often directed toward education if they were interested in religious work. Since women have a long history of professional experience in teaching, this function in the church or synagogue was considered appropriate, as opposed to roles such as preaching. Recently, however, as women take on many responsibilities in their religious communities, those who decide to become religious educators do so because they are drawn to the vocation. One rabbinical student explains how her love of teaching led her to pursue a career as a religious educator.

I was in a teachers' training program, teaching English at a suburban junior high school. Some of the students would talk with me about their upcoming *Bar* and *Bat Mitzvahs* and their Hebrew school. Whenever I had assignments to complete for this training program, I would write curricula for Hebrew schools. Eventually I realized that this was where I really wanted to be . . . my passion was studying about Judaism. I loved teaching about literature. But I felt that I had a real stake in teaching about Judaism, about my history and my heritage. So I started thinking about rabbinical school.

Maybe you, like this student, would like to combine your love of teaching with your love of your faith in a career as a religious educator. Have you had experience teaching in a classroom and felt that it was something you did well? Can you generate enthusiasm for your subject? Would students pay close attention to you? If you are considering this career, you could begin by

133

teaching now. You might volunteer in your congregation to assist a Sunday School teacher, or even teach a class yourself. You might talk with a teacher whose style you admire and ask for advice on how to develop your own skills. Religious educators love teaching and learning about their religious tradition . . . do you? If so, perhaps a career as a religious educator is right for you.

AGENCY STAFF/EXECUTIVE/ADMINISTRATOR

A church or a synagogue represents much more than the congregation that gathers in its building for worship. Through its religious identity, members are connected to many thousands, or even millions, of people of the same tradition. Agencies of the denomination or movement facilitate connections among communities of faith on local, regional, national, and international levels. Those who work in these organizations—both clergy and laity—enable churches and synagogues to accomplish far more through combined resources than they could on their own. The people who staff these organizations are often called agency staff members, executives, or administrators.

What an agency staff member, executive, or administrator does is determined by the position that she holds. For example, a minister who is the director of Native American affairs for her church and helps to educate congregations about social conditions would have very different responsibilities from a rabbi who is a lobbyist for a national organization that represents Jewish interests to members of Congress. While some agency administrators serve their religious community nationally, other staff offer programs, resources, and services locally. Although work based in an office does not fit the traditional picture of what ministers and rabbis do, the agency staff member, executive, or administrator has objectives similar to those of her clergy colleagues in other fields.

A primary goal of religious agencies is to build connections or to network among individuals, communities, and organizations. An administrator spends time in meetings, writing letters, and on the phone as she establishes goals and develops plans to carry them out. If an agency executive has a special focus, such as social action or interfaith relations, she would do research on relevant topics and disseminate the information through articles, programs, workshops, sermons, or seminars. Her work might include fundraising or distribution of funds. She might travel widely to give presentations and attend meetings and conferences. A clergywoman who works in a national staff position in her church comments, "This job requires administrative skills in enabling ideas to become concrete reality. While my position is sometimes thought of as 'bureaucracy,' I believe it can be ministry, and I try to make it such."

Many clergy find that becoming an agency staff member, executive, or administrator is a powerful way to fulfill their religious vocation. They appreciate meeting with diverse groups of people. Their skills and training in pastoral care are essential, as local congregations having difficulties or seeking guidance turn to them for support. Many agency executives enjoy the opportunity to travel; others, especially if they are married or have children, may find that the amount of travel often required is burdensome. Some administrators are grateful for the separation between their professional and personal lives, which is harder to achieve for a rabbi or minister in a congregation. Clergywomen who are mothers may also appreciate schedules that revolve around weekday office hours and usually leave weekends free. Also some clergy in this line of work are glad for the opportunity to focus on a specific concern that is

135

Rev. Laura Sinclair, an American Baptist minister, works for her church nationwide to provide congregations with training and resources.

important to them, such as racial justice or the status of women.

You may discover that agency or administrative work is attractive to you. Are you organized? Do you like reaching out over the phone, through letters, and in person? Does working in an office appeal to you? Do you enjoy making contact with all sorts of people? Do you like to travel? Are you interested in concentrating on a particular concern? Some clergywomen find that agency or administrative work offers them the chance to serve their religious tradition in a way that suits them well personally and professionally. One executive maintains, "I am committed to shaping this institution that it might more clearly reflect God's work in the world." Perhaps as an agency staff member, executive, or administrator you also might also help the organizations of your religion to live out their faith commitments in communities, the nation, and the world.

MISSION WORKER

Today's mission worker addresses the concerns of her church and the world by witnessing to her faith through action. The field of missions has a long history in Christian churches, but no longer does the mission worker emphasize converting people to her religion. Instead she seeks to help others where the church sends her. She earns a subsistence wage and often works in situations of poverty, either in the United States or abroad. The community she serves usually does not have the resources to pay her living expenses and a modest stipend, so they are provided by a congregation or the mission board of her denomination. The personnel and resources of the denomination also support the mission worker in her placement.

Some mission workers today are clergy; some are not. Mission workers who are clergy use their pastoral skills and training as they meet the challenges of their placement. For example, a clergywoman might use her counseling abilities in an inner-city community center, where she would work with people suffering from drug or alcohol addiction. A mission worker might teach at a seminary in Africa. She might be executive director of a home for abused children. Some mission workers are pastors of congregations in developing nations. The field includes a wide variety of vocational options.

Although the work of some mission workers is similar to that of various clergy fields, it is distinguished by the role of the church's mission board. Generally this agency fills requests for mission workers from among those who have applied to serve. When the right person is found, the church "commissions" or entrusts the mission worker to her assignment in a worship service. Some mission programs or positions may be for a limited term of months or years. Other positions seek mission workers who will move to another continent and serve there for a long period of time. For some clergy, mission work is an interlude in their career development that helps them expand their horizons in the church and in the world; for others it is a lifetime commitment.

If you have a sense of adventure, mission work could give you an exciting opportunity to explore other cultures. A mission worker generally lives in the community she serves; sometimes the setting bears little, if any, resemblance to where she grew up. The life-style changes can be startling when the mission worker finds herself in a place where medical care, electricity, and clean water are scarce. Because workers may experience culture shock, mission agencies generally send people to situations that are very different only if they are willing to spend at least a few years in the position. In that way they have time to adjust and carry out their work effectively.

Are you intrigued by the thought of living in another culture? Do you like to take risks, like the chance involved in applying for a mission worker position and going where your church sends you? Are you willing to give up some of the comforts of home in exchange for experiencing the ways of other people? Would you be satisfied with an income that provides for your needs but not much more? Can you help others while respecting and honoring their culture and tradition? Are you open to being transformed by new people and places as you listen and learn? If so, becoming a mission worker might be an exciting opportunity for you.

To find out more about mission possibilities, ask a pastor about your church's mission agency and then get in touch with its personnel department. Inquire about procedures for applying to mission programs and about age regulations. Ask about programs for college students. You may discover that mission work offers you a chance for religious fulfillment and personal adventure.

Guidance from Today's Clergywomen

Being a clergywoman offers many challenges and rewards. Women who are ministers, rabbis, and cantors today know what they appreciate most and like least about their careers. If you have an idea of what to expect as a clergywoman—both the positive and negative aspects of the work—you can proceed with greater confidence. The experiences and insights of these clergywomen may help to guide you as you explore possible paths and advance toward your career goals.

WHAT TO LOOK OUT FOR...

Clergywomen generally love their work, but they do offer some words of caution. "Be careful of your schedule," an agency executive advises, "because overwork is a constant hazard." Many clergywomen echo this warning, noting that they often feel overwhelmed. One congregational minister comments that, while she enjoys the variety of activities in a given day, she is frustrated by never completing her daily list of tasks. A youth minister who works part time also feels burdened by all that she needs to do: "Since I have no set hours, I feel that any spare moment I have should be spent calling youth, or writing a bulletin announcement, or planning an event. I don't take enough time for myself." Clergy who work with congregations tend to agree with a pastor who says, "I don't like being on call twenty-four hours a day." And a rabbi observes, "The hardest part of being a rabbi is never being able to plan. You just don't know when a crisis may arise." A campus minister advises future (and current) clergy-women to be intentional and insistent on making and taking time for themselves.

Even when clergywomen are away from their work the hours are rapidly filled with other demands. Clergywomen who are married or have children often yearn for more time to spend with their families. One pastor observes, "It is difficult to divide my time between the church and my family. I want to give my best to both and it's impossible. Sometimes when I leave for the church I can see that my children are disappointed, and it pulls at my heart." A rabbi agrees, "It's not easy to raise a family (I have two children, now twelve and fifteen) and be there for a congregation seven days a week." An agency executive also feels this tension: "When I used to work with a congregation it created severe conflicts between my professional duties and my desire to be with my husband and children (and to have a little time for myself!). Even in this administrative job I'm called upon to travel frequently and to attend lots of evening meetings. This is very draining, and my family and I both resent the time I miss with them." Clergywomen strive to work out creative solutions in managing their family lives with their professional careers . . . with the help of supportive friends and partners.

Juggling the demands of children while maintaining a career is a challenge that many clergywomen face today.

141

Cantor Martha Novick rehearses for Shabbat services with help from her daughter, Abby.

In our society that is hard for any woman to do, because the culture is not designed to accommodate working mothers (a term that is, in itself, redundant). Maternity leave policies vary widely, and a woman may not be assured of having a few months with her newborn baby before she must return to work if she wants to keep a given position. Some women are even forced to choose between having a child and keeping a job. Day-care options may be expensive or unavailable. Women who do work outside the home often come home to a "second shift" of work *inside* the home, as they provide primary child care and do the shopping, cooking, and cleaning. Even supportive partners who share these responsibilities rarely claim them. And for single mothers, raising a family while maintaining a career is even harder. So how do women do it? With a lot of effort and dedication.

More specifically, the arrangements that a family make to take care of the children (especially when they are small) while the parent(s) work outside the home varies with each individual situation, depending on personal, financial, and professional resources. If a parent can stay at home full time, or if there are two parents with flexible work schedules, a couple may be able to provide the necessary child care themselves. If the parent(s) are lucky enough to live near supportive relatives, a grandparent or a sibling with children may be a great help in taking care of the child or children. A family who can afford to hire a baby-sitter on a steady basis might have someone come into the home or take the child or children to the sitter's house. Sometimes several mothers share a baby-sitter. Educational and enjoyable day-care programs in the neighborhood can provide dependable care while giving children the chance to develop social skills at an early age. New mothers (and fathers) find ways that accommodate their life-style and help them to handle the responsibilities of their career and their family.

How a working woman adjusts to the demands of becoming a parent (or a parent adjusts to the demands of a new career) depends also on her personality. Some women discover when they have children that they want to spend more time with their family than their work allows. If they can afford the cut in salary, they may prefer to work part time for a number of years, especially while the children are little. One rabbi comments, "It's not so bad to take time out to raise a family. I don't want to look back on my life and say, 'I wish I had been with my children more'." A pastor, reflecting on her career and family, says wistfully, "I wish I had had the luxury of being a full-time homemaker for a few years.

143

But my position in the church provided us with housing, so I couldn't afford to leave the ministry for a while." Other clergywomen, however, find that maintaining their career while raising children helps them to be better mothers. One minister asserts, "I love my work. When I feel stimulated and challenged intellectually, I also feel good about myself. Then I appreciate the time with my children more; I am more patient and don't get frustrated as easily." Clergy mothers experiment with different options and then decide what works best for their situation.

Some common frustrations that clergy mothers encounter revolve around educating their faith community. While congregations rarely worry about clergymen who are fathers, clergywomen who are mothers are sometimes perceived as a professional risk. One pastor talks about the interview she had for a position at a church. Someone on the committee wondered if a woman minister could handle the job, and asked her, "What if you became pregnant?" Without skipping a beat, the minister replied, "I'd have a baby." When a minister or rabbi has been working in a position for a few years and then becomes pregnant, the congregation may feel like a jealous older sibling, wondering how much time the new arrival will demand. On the other hand, some congregations gladly welcome the clergyperson's new baby. A community of faith may have unfair expectations of the clergyperson's offspring, whom they expect to model perfect behavior. A clergywoman shows that her family is part of the faith community— not the standard for measuring others.

While clergy mothers may encounter these unique challenges, they also have some advantages over women in other professions. A clergywoman's schedule is usually flexible, allowing her to set her own hours. Thus, she can arrange to be with her child or children when they get home from school, or in an unexpected situation such as illness or injury. The work of a clergywoman is very people-oriented, and she perhaps can be with her child or children as part of her work. For example, a pastor might take her baby with her as she visits older parishioners. A rabbi might lead a retreat for the youth of the synagogue that includes her own children. A clergywoman might take her toddler to her office and set up a playpen. When seeking a baby-sitter, the clergywoman can use contacts in the community to help her find someone reliable. In a church or synagogue that maintains a nursery school (and many do), a clergywoman's child might be part of the program. Some institutions that chaplains serve, such as hospitals or universities, offer day-care centers for employees.

The clergy mother can also grow tired. When a working mother has a career outside the home and maintains the household, one aspect of her life is usually neglected. It is not her performance at work, her care of the children, nor her relationship with her spouse; what suffers most is her care of herself. Women who are overburdened often do not make time for getting exercise, eating well, or sleeping enough. "Watch out that you don't get run over by your life," a clergy mother cautions; "if you do, you're no good to anyone—not to your congregation, your family, or yourself."

Clergywomen without the responsibilities of marriage or motherhood face other challenges. Clergy who are divorced (whether they are mothers or not) may feel unfairly judged by their congregation. Some women report feeling lonely and isolated. One minister comments, "As the pastor, I am always the 'other' in the community, even though I'm loved." Another clergywoman adds, "I move every few years; it can be hard to maintain relationships." A young pastor honestly admits, "I have a very difficult time trying to find a man

145

who is open and understanding enough to marry a clergywoman." A church administrator says that getting to know people outside of work can be hard, and observes, "Stereotypes are not much fun—neither the ones that make you saintly and in direct communication with God, nor the ones that make you just a weirdo." Women clergy are changing these social stereotypes.

Perhaps not surprisingly, many married clergywomen are married to clergymen. An extensive contemporary study of Protestant clergywomen reveals that over half of the married clergywomen surveyed were part of a clergy couple. While in seminary, future ministers, rabbis, and cantors—women and men—naturally become friends. When two people in the same career field fall in love and decide to commit themselves to each other, they can easily understand the demands of their partner's career. However, the clergy couple may have a hard time negotiating placements in the same field in the same area at the same time. One rabbi reveals, "I'm glad I married a lawyer. It's easier to work out our careers together. Besides, I like talking about something besides temple." Conversely, another pastor says, "I don't know how I could be married to someone who isn't in ministry. My husband relates to what I go through." Of course, if you are considering a future with a partner, you cannot predict whom you might fall in love with, but you *can* choose a spouse who supports you and encourages you in what you want to do with your life.

As many clergywomen pursue what they want to do with their lives, they encounter discrimination because of their gender. "I'm tired of being told, 'You don't *look* like a minister,' or 'I don't believe in lady preachers,'" a hospital chaplain laments. "What I like least about being a clergywoman," a pastor adds, "is feeling that I am expected to prove my ability and faith more than male clergy. I am seen as a little less than a clergy*man* in the eyes of so many." A minister says, "Most people will say, 'I'll give her a chance, but if I don't like her . . .', which I don't think is the general attitude toward clergymen." Another clergywoman, who works as a copastor with a male colleague, reports, "People call up and when I answer the phone, sometimes they ask to 'speak to the *real* minister.'" Such comments reflect a sexist attitude that makes the clergywoman's job much harder.

Clergywomen of color or with disabilities often suffer additional discrimination. One minister describes her experience: "As a black clergywoman, I have often been the recipient of anger, hostility, and resentment from my white *women* and men peers, who think things are 'easy' for me. It is angering and hurtful." An aspiring clergywoman who uses a wheelchair says that her struggle to be ordained is "an arduous and endless journey of frustration." She recounts how the hierarchy of her church rejected her because she was "different," implying that it was "wrong." "The bishop decided that I was thumbs down, 'unemployable.' And that was that," she says. Yet she has not given up on her quest to be ordained. "Despite all this, I *know* that it *will* happen someday." Her courage attests to the strength of many women who counter prejudice with persistence.

Some clergywomen find that the expectations placed on them are excessive. One pastor comments, "I don't like having to prove myself because I am a woman. It is a challenge to be careful because I am the first woman, often, that people meet in the ministry, and I know they will judge other women by their opinion of me and my style. It seems unfair, yet it's human nature." Another minister feels that she is expected to "fit into a pre-set concept of what others think I should be." A pastor

147

says, "I dislike it when others look to me as a model of perfection; some parishioners have impossibly high expectations." One minister resents "having responsibility for overseeing everything." And a rabbi finds spiritual demands overwhelming: "I don't like it when people assume that I have the answers to life's ugliest questions—like, 'Why do children suffer and die?'."
Perhaps one minister sums up the difficulty as she reflects, "The hardest thing is to realize when others' expectations of you (or your own, for that matter) are unrealistic, and to have enough courage and honesty to admit it." Then she adds, "I hoped I was superwoman in the beginning, but experience clipped my cape!"

These concerns of clergywomen are not intended to "clip your cape" even before you start soaring; rather they are to help you gain an honest understanding of problems that clergywomen work through. A lot would be required of you in this career, and often the pay is modest. Ministers and their families sometimes struggle financially, especially if the minister's salary is the sole means of support. Nonetheless, clergywomen enjoy their careers, and many agree with the pastor who declares, "I love being in ministry!"

WHAT TO LOOK FORWARD TO...

As a clergywoman, you would believe in what you do. Because the demands are so extensive, both in preparation and in the work that a rabbi, minister, or cantor does, clergywomen are clearly dedicated to their vocations. Believing that your occupation truly makes a difference is a strong and compelling reward. A rabbi says, "I have the satisfaction of doing work that has some significance and helps make the world a better place." And a minister affirms, "I love having the privilege of spending my work hours focused on stuff that matters: God, responding to God's call, caring for others, and building community."

Clergywomen are closely involved with the people in the community they serve, and they understand that the relationships they form are precious. "I like being intimately involved in people's lives so that I laugh with them and cry with them," a congregational minister says. People often approach their minister or rabbi at pivotal moments in their lives—whether joyous celebrations of a wedding or new baby, or tragic occasions of a brutal victimization or an unexpected death. Offering spiritual strength, practical counsel, joyful affirmation, or crisis intervention, the clergyperson helps to guide people through these times of change and challenge. She becomes an integral part of their lives and remains in their memories of this special time. A prison chaplain says that she sees people healed of "pain, guilt, and lack of self-confidence. . . . Prisoners come to express their love of God by a glow on their face and service in their own kinds of ministry. I feel blessed to help enable them to experience this grace-filled transformation." One pastor notes, "I appreciate the opportunity to be with people in all the 'holy moments' of their lives—birth, death, pain, and joy. Together we celebrate God's gift of life to us all."

Being a clergywoman also offers flexibility in one's schedule and variety in one's tasks. Ministers, rabbis, and cantors appreciate the freedom to determine, to a great extent, what they do with their days. Says one pastor, "I like the opportunities to be self-directed, managing my time through my priorities rather than policy or supervisory directives." If an important concern arises, such as a tragedy in the community, or if the clergywoman has a personal problem, such as a sick child, she can usually accommodate her schedule accordingly. A rabbi appreciates this diversity and comments, "I enjoy the fact that each day is different, each a challenge—sometimes frustrating, often exhilarating." And a hospital chaplain adds, "It's never boring!"

Clergywomen feel stimulated by their work both personally and professionally, since who they are and what they do are intertwined. "I get to use different skills and do what I love most—study, teach, preach, pray—while interacting with people of all ages, cultures, and backgrounds," a congregational minister says. A campus chaplain expands on the point:

> I love so much of this vocation that it's hard to single out what I like most. I love the preaching, sharing in worship with a community yearning for wholeness; I love teaching, sharing the truth as I have discerned it and helping others discern what truth God is revealing to them; I love walking with people through the valleys and mountaintops, discovering the sacred moments and God in our midst. Most of all, I love the way ministry uses so much of who I am—all my gifts, talents, and skills find their fullest expression in this vocation. That is so life-giving and makes life so exciting and wonder-filled.

Other clergywomen share this chaplain's enthusiasm. They enjoy working with "faithful, loving people" who also seek to grow spiritually. They cherish the support and friendship of clergywomen they know; one cantor describes her colleagues as "a wonderfully creative group of people." Clergywomen are respected as valuable contributors to society. They cherish their religious traditions and feel committed to the future of their community of faith.

While advancing into the next century, clergywomen are still pioneers. As a result, one minister points out, a clergywoman has "...the freedom to think and act critically and independently." Because most people picture a man as a stereotypical clergyperson, women are not associated with images of clergy as somber and authoritative. A congregational pastor observes, "I think people are still somewhat intrigued with women as clergy, and, as a result, they listen harder to us. They don't expect us to be 'typical.'" And a Korean clergywoman asserts, "I am bringing more awareness of clergywomen to the Korean church. It's difficult, but I see it as a challenge being somewhat of a pioneer in the Korean church. I'm opening new possibilities, especially for young Korean women. We can be clergy and it's great!"

Despite the difficulties, most women rabbis, ministers, and cantors would agree with this Korean pastor's affirmation. They find their daily work stimulating and interesting while they help others in meaningful ways. Clergywomen have the freedom to choose what they emphasize in their vocation, whether it be counseling, teaching, preaching, administering, or programming. They learn and grow along with those they serve. Perhaps most important, a clergywoman's work is practical but also deeply spiritual. As one clergywoman says, "I feel fulfilled personally, professionally, and spiritually. Being a clergywoman is a privilege and a joy."

SUCCESS IN REACHING YOUR GOALS...

Many clergywomen join in offering a piece of advice that sounds simple but proves to be challenging in their own lives. "Be realistic," they suggest. Should you become a clergywoman, as you work toward the goal— and once you achieve it—be fair with yourself. Offer your skills confidently, but at the same time do not expect too much of yourself. "Overworking backfires," a rabbi observes, "because you get too tired and 'burned out' to be productive. Don't try to do it all, and don't expect to become rich or famous." And a pastoral counselor suggests the value of learning time-management skills, adding, "Know your limits." "It is hard to obtain success simultaneously in all areas of your life," a religious educator notes. "Sometimes either career advancement or family life goes on a slower track for a few years." And a hospital chaplain cautions, "Don't drive yourself into the ground trying to be superwoman/ superpastor/supermom/superanything. It won't work." To avoid this trap of attempting to do too much, a rabbi reminds future clergywomen, "Don't take praise or criticism too seriously. You cannot please everyone, but you can please yourself."

While caring for others, clergywomen need to care for themselves. "Stay in shape physically," a cantor advises, "regular workouts are vital for my sanity and physical stamina." A pastor reminds future clergywomen, "Take time to read, contemplate, and reflect on your work. And make time for pure fun." To avoid feeling isolated, some clergywomen join or create a support group of colleagues. Build trusting relationships, both with personal friends and professional coworkers. You need to know that there are people you can turn to, when so many are turning to you.

If you love people and your religious tradition, you might love a career as a clergywoman. Should this become your vocation, a minister advises, "Enjoy your work . . . and make sure to keep your sense of humor." To have a satisfying personal life and fulfilling work is a blessing. Many women are grateful for the blessing that they find in their careers as clergy.

9

Getting Started . . . Now!

Exciting opportunities lie ahead. The accomplishments of yesterday's and today's clergywomen have created new possibilities for you. At this point in your life, future career choices may seem limitless and perhaps a bit overwhelming. The best way to investigate further whether becoming a clergywoman is right for you is to start exploring the career now!

An important first step is simply to talk with clergy. You might begin with the minister or rabbi of your congregation to find out what she or he does. Conversations with various clergypeople can help you understand what their careers involve. If you are interested in becoming a chaplain, investigate the possibilities in your own community. Does the local hospital have a pastoral care department? How far is the nearest prison? Is there a college campus in your area? Maybe you could arrange a meeting with the chaplain(s) to talk and even visit where they work. Most clergy are happy to talk with someone who is considering becoming a clergyperson, although you should not be discouraged if he or she is unable to schedule a meeting right away. When you do get together, have a list of questions. What does this clergyperson do in an average day? What does she or he like best or least about the work? Honest responses to your questions can help you decide whether you would like the career.

You may want to talk specifically with clergywomen about the struggles they face and the joys they experience in the vocation. Perhaps your pastor or rabbi is a woman. If your clergyperson is a man, ask him if he knows any women colleagues. You might also look in the phone book under "Community Information" for the listings of churches and synagogues. Are there any women among the names of clergy? Give them a call and request a meeting. This takes some assertiveness, but you have nothing to lose.

One clergywoman describes a time when she was in high school and called up a woman minister who had just moved into the area.

> I was nervous, but I called up this woman and told her that I was thinking about becoming a minister. I had only met her once very briefly, but I asked if we could get together sometime. She was very nice and asked me if I wanted to meet her for lunch. So we set a date and a few weeks later we got together at a diner. Over burgers and french fries, I asked her some questions. She was very honest in her responses, and while she told me that being a minister wasn't easy, she said it was worth it and encouraged me to seek ordination. That was over a decade ago, and now she and I are colleagues. I see her at meetings from time to time, and I smile when I remember our diner conversation.

If you get to know current clergywomen, you may encounter someone who is doing what you would like to do and can serve as a role model. You might even seek out a mentor to guide you in your spiritual and professional development. One clergywoman advises,

"Find a mentor—having one makes all the difference!"

You can also discover what clergy do by getting involved in your faith community. Take an active role in your home congregation. You might teach a Sunday school class or be an assistant teacher. Sing in the choir and learn about sacred music. Volunteer for a committee and offer your input. Join in the youth group— or start one—and take a leadership role. Perhaps you could write an article or a column for your church newsletter or synagogue bulletin. Offer to do a reading in a worship service. Participate in a service led by the youth, or suggest working with the minister or rabbi to organize one. Maybe you could be the preacher! Experiences with your congregation can help you decide whether you would like to lead a congregation yourself.

Also look for opportunities for service in your community. Are there agencies, organizations, or institutions that appeal to you? Volunteer programs often provide the chance to try out a field. For example, if you are intrigued by prison chaplaincy, you might volunteer to collect needed items for inmates at a local jail. If you want to find out more about hospital chaplaincy, you might volunteer at a nearby hospital. You could learn about work with children by becoming a "big brother" or "big sister." If there is a peer counseling program in your school or community center, you could develop counseling skills. By volunteering with a program that delivers meals to people who are home-bound, you could learn about pastoral care. Investigate the resources of your community, and then find a way to participate in what interests you.

Summers also provide fun and engaging ways to continue your career exploration. Find out about the religious camps of your denomination or movement. Perhaps you could work as a counselor or counselor-in-training. Any job that puts you in the environment,

155

even working in the kitchen or as a lifeguard, would help you learn about your religion in refreshing ways. If your congregation offers summer youth programs such as a Vacation Church School, you could volunteer to help. You might spend a summer in Israel to delve into your religious heritage. Maybe there are youth conferences or seminars that you could attend. Some agencies and organizations that offer volunteer/study/ work programs are listed in the Appendix. Keep looking for possibilities, and you are sure to find some.

You also need to look inside yourself. Build your personal faith and your love of your religious heritage. You might talk about God and the world with people you trust. Some clergywomen find that keeping a "spiritual journal" in which they write the thoughts, feelings, events, problems, joys, and questions of their lives helps them to clarify their choices. Perhaps you might be guided through prayer. As one clergywoman advises, "Don't let society or tradition judge who you are. God created you. God knows you. Trust God."

If you keep your mind and your heart open, you will discover what is right for you. As you grow spiritually, physically, intellectually, socially, and professionally, have the confidence to be yourself. Enjoy your career exploration, because it really is exciting to decide what you will do with your life. At the same time, know that it is okay to be confused. Ask a lot of questions. Perhaps someday a career as a clergywoman will be deeply meaningful for you, as it is for thousands of women now. One of those thousands of clergywomen offers this advice:

Think about becoming a clergywoman. Pray about it a lot. If the ministry seems like a place where you can do good work for others and also nourish yourself, then by all means—go for it. And try not to be bound by other people's conceptions of clergy. We're creating something new as we go along.

Appendix

**Approximate Percentages of Women Clergy in the
Early 1990s**

	Percentage of *total clergy*
Protestant Denominations	
African Methodist Episcopal (AME) Zion	30%
American Baptist Church	9%
Christian Church (Disciples of Christ)	14%
Episcopal Church	9%
Evangelical Lutheran Church in America	12%
Presbyterian Church (USA)	11%
United Church of Christ	18%
United Methodist Church	13%

Branches of Judaism	*Cantors*	*Rabbis*
Reform	25%	10%
Reconstructionist	*	32%
Conservative	**	4%

---

* The Reconstructionist movement does not invest cantors;
however, cantors invested in other movements serve in
Reconstructionist synagogues.

** Women cantors in the Conservative movement were first
invested in 1987. Percentage unavailable.

QUESTIONNAIRES

To gather information and insights for this book, the following questionnaires were sent to Protestant, Jewish, and Roman Catholic women across the country.

CAREERS FOR WOMEN AS CLERGY

To Protestant Women:
1. How would you describe your ministry?
   Congregational ministry   *Solo Cosenior Asst/Assoc*
   Hospital chaplaincy
   Campus ministry
   Pastoral counseling
   Teaching/religious
      education
   Prison chaplaincy
   Mission
   Agency
   Administrative
   Other *(please specify)* _____

2. How would you describe the community in which you work? (urban, suburban, rural, race, economic bracket, etc.)

3. What do your responsibilities include?

4. What might an average day entail?

5. Is ministry your first career?
   If not, what other career(s) have you pursued (please include homemaking) and for how many years before you were ordained?

6. How many years have you been ordained?

7. How would you describe your call to ministry?

8. What do you like most about being a clergywoman?

159

9. What do you like least about being a clergywoman?

10. What advice would you offer to a young woman considering your field?

Please feel free to add any other thoughts, comments, stories, or suggestions.

To Jewish Women

1. What is your role serving the Jewish community?
   Congregational rabbi   *Solo Co-Senior Asst/Assoc*
   Cantor
   Hospital chaplain
   Campus chaplain
   Pastoral counselor
   Teaching/religious
      educator
   Prison chaplain
   Agency
   Administrative
   Other *(please specify)* _____

2. How would you describe the community in which you work? (urban, suburban, rural, race, economic bracket, etc.)

3. What do your responsibilities include?

4. What might an average day entail?

5. Is this your first career?
   If not, what other career(s) have you pursued (please include homemaking) and for how many years before you were ordained?

6. How many years have you been ordained?

7. What motivated you to seek the rabbinate/cantorate as your career?

8. What do you like most about being a clergywoman?

9. What do you like least about being a clergywoman?

10. What advice would you offer to a young woman considering your field?

Please feel free to add any other thoughts, comments, stories, or suggestions.

To Roman Catholic Women

1. How would you describe your ministry?
   Parish associate
   Hospital chaplaincy
   Pastoral counseling
   Prison chaplaincy
   Campus ministry
   Religious
   Mission
   Teaching/religious education
   Diocesan work
   Community organizing
   Other *(please specify)* _____

2. How long have you been involved in this work?

3. How would you describe the community you serve? (urban, suburban, rural, race, economic bracket, etc.)

4. Do you work in this ministry full time or part time?

5. Are you a volunteer or paid?

6. What do your responsibilities include?

7. What might an average day entail?

8. How would you describe your vocation or call?

9. What do like best about what you do?

10. What do you like least about what you do?

11. What advice would you offer to a young woman considering your field?

12. How do you feel about the ordination of women in the Roman Catholic Church?

13. Do you believe that this will ever happen?
    If so, do you expect to see the ordination of women in the Roman Catholic Church within your lifetime? Why or why not?

Please feel free to add any other thoughts, comments, stories, or suggestions.

The end of the questionnaires read:
The following information is optional but will help if I have further questions and will also help to insure religious and racial inclusivity.

Your name _____

Address _____
         street   town   state   zip

Phone _____

Race/Ethnicity _____

Religious Affiliation/Denomination/Movement _____

SCHOLARSHIP RESOURCES

Many local congregations and organizations give scholarships to college or seminary students. Religious, civic, and women's groups in your community may have scholarships available. Some national offices also offer scholarships and low-interest loans, with certain funds especially designated for ethnic students. You can obtain information about financial resources for studies through the following offices:

American Baptist
Educational Ministries
Financial Aid Office
American Baptist Churches USA
PO Box 851
Valley Forge, PA 19482-0851
(215) 768-2000

Christian Church (Disciples of Christ)
Scholarship Information *(for graduate studies)*
Center for Leadership and Ministry
Christian Church (Disciples of Christ)
PO Box 1986
Indianapolis, IN 46206
(317) 353-1491

Episcopal
Office of Asian-American / Black / Hispanic / Native American Ministries *(separate offices)*
or
Board for Theological Education *(listing of scholarship resources)*
Episcopal Church Center
815 Second Avenue
New York, NY 10017
(800) 334-7626 (outside NY state)
(800) 321-2231 (in NY state)

Evangelical Lutheran Church in America
Department for Theological Education
Division of Ministry
Evangelical Lutheran Church in America
8765 West Higgins Road
Chicago, IL 60631-4195
(312) 380-2873

Presbyterian Church (USA)
Office of Financial Aid for Studies
Presbyterian Church (USA)
100 Witherspoon Street
Louisville, KY 40202-1396
(502) 569-5745

United Church of Christ
Minority Fellowship Program *(for ethnic students)*
United Church of Christ
700 Prospect Avenue
Cleveland, OH 44115-1110
(216) 736-3787

United Methodist Church
Office of Loans and Scholarships
General Board of Higher Education and Ministry
United Methodist Church
P.O. Box 871
Nashville, TN 37202-0871
(615) 340-7344

for ethnic students
National Division Committee on Scholarships
General Board of Global Ministries
United Methodist Church
475 Riverside Drive
New York, NY 10115

VOLUNTEER/STUDY/WORK PROGRAMS

Jewish

American Jewish Society for Service *(summer work-camps for high school students)*
15 East 26th Street
New York, NY 10010
(212) 683-6178

American Pardes Foundation *(academic program in Israel)*
644 Humphrey Street
PO Box 1
Swampscott, MA 01907
(617) 592-4542

American Zionist Youth Foundation (AZYF) *(volunteer/study/work programs in Israel)*
University Student Department
110 East 59th Street
New York, NY 10022-1373
1-800-27-ISRAEL

Christian

Episcopal Church Volunteers for Mission *(long-term volunteer programs)*
Episcopal Church Center
815 Second Avenue
New York, NY 10017
(212) 922-5326

International Christian Youth Exchange *(summer workcamps abroad)*
Short-Term Programs
134 West 26th Street
New York, NY 10001
(212) 206-7307

165

Lutheran Volunteer Corps *(one-year volunteer programs)*
1226 Vermont Avenue NW
Washington, DC 20005
(202) 387-3222

Mennonite Central Committee *(long-term and short-term volunteer programs)*
21 South 12th Street
Akron, PA 17501-0500
(717) 859-1151

Mission Volunteers/USA *(long-term and short-term volunteer programs)*
Presbyterian Church (USA)
100 Witherspoon Street
Louisville, KY 40202-1396
(502) 569-5295

Mission Personnel Resources Program Department *(volunteer service programs)*
General Board of Global Ministries
United Methodist Church
475 Riverside Drive
New York, NY 10115
(212) 870-3659
1-800-654-5929 (outside NY state)

Interfaith and secular
Council on International Educational Exchange (CIEE) *(volunteer clearinghouse)*
205 East 42nd Street
New York, NY 10017
(212) 661-1414

Published Volunteer Guides:

Terry, Max (ed.). *Volunteer! The Comprehensive Guide to Voluntary Service in the U.S. and Abroad.* New York: Council on International Educational Exchange, 1992.

Driver, David E. *The Good Heart Book: A Guide to Volunteering.* Chicago: Noble, 1989.

CHAPLAINCY ORGANIZATIONS

Association of Clinical Pastoral Education, Inc. (*interfaith*)
1549 Clairmont Road
Decatur, GA 30033
(404) 320-1472

B'nai B'rith Hillel Foundations
1640 Rhode Island Avenue, NW
Washington, DC 20036
(202) 857-6560

College of Chaplains, Inc. (*interfaith*)
1701 East Woodfield Road
Schaumburg, IL 60713
(708) 240-1014

National Association of Catholic Chaplains
3501 South Lake Drive
PO Box 07473
Milwaukee, WI 53207-0473
(414) 483-4898

National Association of Jewish Chaplains
10 East 73rd Street
New York, NY 10021

Glossary

clergy Persons ordained (ministers, priests, and rabbis) or invested as religious officials (cantors).

denomination Religious group or sect (term used in Protestantism).

ecumenical Promoting or fostering Christian unity.

interfaith Involving persons of different religions.

Judaica The entire body of Jewish knowledge, literature, and customs.

laity Collectively, people who are not members of the clergy.

liturgy Religious ritual; worship service; elements of such a service.

mainline Protestant denominations having an established position.

ministry The service or profession of a religious person.

movement A religious group or sect (term used in Judaism); also called *branch*.

ordain To give authority as a minister, priest, or rabbi.

sacrament A rite of a religion, such as baptism or communion.

seminary A school for the study of religion and theology; usually a graduate school.

secular Pertaining to worldly things; not religious.

theology The study of God and of one's relationship with God.

Bibliography

Andrews, William L., ed. *Sisters of the Spirit: Three Black Women's Autobiographies of the Nineteenth Century*. Bloomington: Indiana University Press, 1986.

Bloom, Naomi. *Contributions of Women—Religion*. Minneapolis, MN: Dillon, 1978.

Carroll, Jackson W.; Hargrove, Barbara; and Lummis, Adair T. *Women of the Cloth: A New Opportunity for the Churches*. San Francisco: Harper and Row, 1983.

Clinebell, Howard. *Basic Types of Pastoral Care and Counseling*. Nashville: Abingdon, 1984.

Gottschalk, Alfred. *To Learn and to Teach: Your Life as a Rabbi*. New York: Rosen, 1988.

Greenberg, Simon, ed. *The Ordination of Women as Rabbis: Studies and Responsa*. New York: The Jewish Theological Seminary of America, 1988.

Heyward, Carter. *A Priest Forever: The Formation of a Woman and a Priest*. New York: Harper and Row, 1976.

Jacquet, Constant H. Jr., ed. *Yearbook of American and Canadian Churches 1990*. Nashville: Abingdon, 1990.

Kenneally, James K. *The History of American Catholic Women*. New York: Crossroad, 1990.

Lehman, Edward C. Jr. *Women Clergy: Breaking Through Gender Barriers*. New Brunswick, NJ: Transaction, 1985.

MacHaffie, Barbara. *Her Story: Women in Christian Tradition*. Philadelphia: Fortress, 1986.

Marcus, Jacob Rader. *The American Jewish Woman. 1654–1980*. New York: KTAV, 1981.

Poling, Nancy Werking, with Ortiz, Gloria Claudia, illustrator. *Most Ministers Wear Sneakers*. New York: Pilgrim, 1991.

Portnoy, Mindy Avra, with Rubin, Steffi Karen, illustrator. *Ima on the Bima: My Mommy Is a Rabbi*. Rockville, MD: Kar-Ben Copies, 1986.

Priesand, Sally. *Judaism and the New Woman*. New York: Behrman, 1975.

Ruether, Rosemary, and McLaughlin, Eleanor, eds. *Women of Spirit: Female Leadership in the Jewish and Christian Traditions*. New York: Simon and Schuster, 1979.

Ruether, Rosemary Radford, and Keller, Rosemary Skinner, eds. *Women and Religion: Volume One—The Nineteenth Century*. San Francisco: Harper and Row, 1981.

———. *Women and Religion: Volume Two—The Colonial and Revolutionary Periods*. San Francisco: Harper and Row, 1983.

———. *Women and Religion: Volume Three—1900–1968*. San Francisco: Harper and Row, 1986.

Schaper, Donna. *Common Sense About Men and Women in the Ministry*. Washington, D.C.: Alban Institute, 1990.

Schockley, Donald G. *Campus Ministry: The Church Beyond Itself*. Louisville, KY: Westminster/John Knox, 1989.

Index